Soul Numerology

Soul
Numerology

Julie Gale

Thorsons
An Imprint of HarperCollins*Publishers*

Thorsons
An Imprint of HarperCollins*Publishers*
77–85 Fulham Palace Road,
Hammersmith, London W6 8JB

Published by Thorsons 1998
10 9 8 7 6 5 4 3 2 1

A catalogue record for this book
is available from the British Library

ISBN 0 7225 3788 3

Printed and bound in Great Britain by
Woolnough Bookbinding Limited,
Irthlingborough, Northamptonshire

Grateful thanks to

Brenda Miller of Teignmouth and Jenny Bradbury of Stanley, Scotland, for their kind reading and correcting of the manuscript of this book, and the College of Psychic Studies for their encouragement.

This book is dedicated to my husband, Philip, for his encouragement and help over the years in checking my numbers.

Contents

Introduction

'I wish I could find out what my Soul Path is,' people often say to me. 'I'd like to know what my life lessons are, and if I have any of whatever this thing is called "Karma".'

You don't have to go through life not knowing who you are or why you are here. As I tell audiences in the lecture I give called *Reading the Soul*, the answers to these questions are written in many ways and places – you just need to know how and where to look.

Those of us born into the Western tradition have had it drummed into us that 'it is not ours to know' or 'only God knows' – even when it comes to our deeper selves we have been forbidden all methods of divining. The Eastern traditions are much wiser about such things, but in our culture these methods were consigned to the realms of 'evil', and either went underground or were used to tell vapid fortunes for those only interested in tall dark strangers or material gain.

I use the word 'divine' with purpose. I feel that the 'Divine' – in whatever form you care to think of It/Him/Her – took great care to construct various methods which we could use to seek out what we want to know about ourselves. These methods are sometimes called Occult Sciences. I prefer to think of them as tools to help us discover ourselves.

I myself, other than having opened up mediumship, healing and channelling in myself, have never tried to learn any of these 'tools' that people use when interested in things of an alternative or occult nature. Astrology I found too difficult to learn in the days before computers, and I still get my astrologer friends to read my chart for me. With Palmistry I could never remember which line was which, as for Graphology – well, all those slants and hooks, above or below the line – and I had never even looked at a pack of Tarot cards until fairly recently.

I went on like this for well over 25 years, dismissing all the occult tools, until I went on an 'Aura-Soma' colour reading course where I was taught something called 'Soul Therapy'. This is a system of getting people to make four choices from dozens of double-coloured bottles of oil. From this one was taught to 'read' the colours. I was fascinated to find it could give so much information: where the soul had come from, what its life purpose was, and so on.

This course spoke about 'The Masters' – a notion based on the theosophical model of 'The Masters'. I was a little unsure about this side of things and asked to be pointed to a book that might tell me more. One was suggested and I managed to lay hold of a copy. The book had indeed something to say about these Masters, but was based on *numerology*, not colours. I fear the colour readings slipped into second place once I'd discovered the fascinating study of numbers and their meanings.

Like most people, I had vaguely worked out 'my number' from my date of birth after reading a magazine article on the subject; in the same way one finds out what astrological sign one is. But it had never struck me so forcibly as now. This book, plus others on numerology, opened up my life and laid it out before me like nothing had ever done before. It answered questions as to the 'whys and wherefores' of the many strange and bizarre happenings in my life, and so much more. I am sure any of the other methods would have done the same thing, but this one worked for me. I knew I had found the right tool.

There are many good books that will show you workings and meanings of numerology. I recommend some of them at the end of this book for further study. Like them, this book will teach you the basics for working out your numbers – but it is in the *interpretation* of the meanings and their application that you will find a difference. As the title suggests, I lean mostly towards the divination of a person's spiritual life and character, life path and lessons.

Let's make a start by finding out how to discover your basic number. I wish you a very happy journey of discovery.

Julie Gale

How to Use This Book

Some people dip into books, while others work through from start to finish. I have arranged this book to be read through once from start to finish, but after that it can be dipped into to find a particular section or aspect of numerology, as needed.

Some chapters have plenty of actual numerology for you to get your teeth into, but others are more in the way of explanation. As each method of how to find a particular number is given, so you will find a chart of meanings. For instance, once we have worked out how to find the Birth Number, at the end of the chapter you will find a chart of meaning for each possible Birth Number.

You may then work your own chart out as you progress through the book, and later, when you work out other people's charts, you can go from chapter to chapter always finding the relevant paragraph to help you.

In this way you may work out a chart for anyone without the trouble of remembering all the meanings. Later you will find it becomes second nature to remember the relevance of each number. I hope you will eventually have the confidence to give a reading without using just the meanings given in this book, adding your own garnered experience and insight to your interpretations.

part one

The Meanings of the Numbers

Numerologists use the numbers 1-2-3-4-5-6-7-8-9, 11 and 22. There follow the basic meanings for these numbers. Some numerologists use 33, 44, and the other 'double numbers' going up, but we will just stay with 11 and 22, which are known as *Master Numbers*.

Not all numerologists agree about these meanings, and as you delve into the subject you will find new meanings for yourself.

These meanings tend to relate to people's characteristics and types, not always, but mostly. Later I will enlarge on these meanings.

1 Individuality, Leadership, Pioneer Spirit, One Alone, Selflessness

2 Partnership, Power Behind the Throne, Diplomatic, Sensitive

3 Communication, Joy of Life, Expression, Socially Skilful

4 Hard Working, Successful Despite Limitations, Orderly

5 Freedom, Seeing What Is Over the Hill, Purposeful

6 Love, Family, Balance, Responsibility, Home-loving

7 Psychic, Mystic, Intuitive, Analytical, Different

8 Material Success, Business-minded, Worldly Goods

9 Humanitarian, Generous, Helper, Alternative Ideas

11 Mystic, Intuitive, Illumination, Bright Ideas, Dreamer

22 Potential Power to Build, Creativity, Adeptness

Finding Your Birth Number

How do the meanings outlined in the previous section apply to you? In the first instance simply by adding up your date of birth by the most simple method, as in this example:

John was born on the 23/6/1946

So we add up each individual number like this:

2 + 3 + 6 + 1 + 9 + 4 + 6 = 31.

Now we add the two numbers in 31 (3 + 1) together, which equals 4.

So John would be a 4.

Whatever you are asked to do with a given set of numbers to bring them down to a single number is referred to as 'Reducing' your numbers. I call the 'Reduced' date of birth number the Birth Number. It relates to the life path of the subject of the reading. You may find it called Life Path in other books, or even something else again. I find it easier to remember words that state exactly what it is.

Let's do it again:

Jane was born on the 1/11/1911

We add up these numbers 1 + 1 + 1 + 1 + 9 + 1 + 1 = 15

Again, we add up 1 + 5 together, which equals 6.

So Jane would be a 6.

Now reduce your own birth number.

This then is the simplest method of working out a Birth Number.

Returning to John as a 4 and consulting our list of meanings of numbers, he would be likely to be a hard worker, very orderly, but suffer from limitations being put on his life. Jane, as a 6, would be likely to be family-orientated, liking things to be in a balanced state, and very loving.

But this method of addition can miss out some very important pointers, so I am going to give you another method of reducing the Birth Number which will still add up to the same number but give us some additional information.

Please Note
I will use this second method in all calculations for the remainder of this book.

We will use the same birth dates as before. John was born on 23/6/1946. This time we do not add straight across the whole date but reduce each part of the date, placing the figures below the date and working downwards like this:

$$\downarrow 23 \ldots\ldots / \ldots 6 \ldots / \ldots 1946$$
$$\downarrow 2+3 \ldots / \ldots 6 \ldots / \ldots 1+9+4+6$$
$$\downarrow 5 \ldots\ldots / \ldots 6 \ldots / \ldots 20 \text{ (so } 2+0) = 2$$

Now we add across: $\rightarrow 5 \ldots\ldots + \ldots 6 \ldots + \ldots 2 = 13 \ldots \text{(and } 1+3) = 4$
Birth Number = 4

Take note of the double number of 13 because it will become very important later. You will note that it is not the same as the one arrived at by the first, simple method. By adding together (13) 1 + 3 we arrive at the same Birth Number for John as we had previously, namely a 4. *But* we write this as 13/4, and assign John the Birth Number 13/4. This particular double number alerts me to issues that John must deal with in this life. (We will go into more detail about this we have covered a little more ground work.)

Now let's do Jane's numbers by the second method for practice.
Remember Jane was born on the 1/11/1911.

$$\downarrow 1 \ldots\ldots / \ldots 11 \ldots / \ldots 1911$$
$$\downarrow 1 \ldots\ldots / \ldots 11 \ldots / \ldots 1+9+1+1 = 12$$
$$\downarrow 1 \ldots\ldots / \ldots 11 \ldots / \ldots 12 \text{ (so } 1+2) = 3$$

Now we add across: $\rightarrow 1 \ldots\ldots + \ldots 11 \ldots + \ldots 3 = 15 \text{ (and } 1+5) = 6$
Birth Number = 6

So Jane is a 15/6. Here we come across the rule about Master Number. Did you notice I did not add the 1 and 1 of her 11 together? That is because 11 is a Master Number. If a number reduces down to 11 or 22 then you use the 11 or 22 and do not reduce it any further. That is, you do not add 1 + 1 or 2 + 2 except in rare circumstances which I will tell you about as we reach them. So for those born in November, the month always stays an 11, and for those with birthdays on the 11th or 22nd, the number always stays the 11 or 22.

Having said this, the year 1911 is *not* divided 1 + 9 + 11 – the 1s are added separately. This is because the number is really 1,911, not 19 and 11.

So our Jane is a 15/6. Remember, this would mean she is likely to be family-orientated, like things to be in a balanced state and be very loving.

So now you can reduce a date of birth and get not just basic, but also most important information about the subject of the reading. Reduce your own date of birth by this second method, and then reduce the dates listed below. These are all famous people's dates of birth whose names I will give you later on. Also, practise reducing any dates of people you know, and compare the result with what you know of their personalities.

5/5/1818	6/8/1881	22/2/1857
15/8/1950	14/3/1879	27/1/1756
3/12/1923	30/11/1874	18/6/1942
15/4/1452	25/10/1881	

Here is a Workout Chart for you to copy and use:

Birth Date ..↓......./......./........
 ..↓......./......./........
 ↓......./......./........
Now we add across: → ....+.......+........♥ ____(**Birth Number**)

Here it is filled out with John's details:

Birth Date 23......./...6..../..1946
 5......./...6..../..20
Now we add across: → 5.......+....6...+ 2 = 13 ♥ 4 (**Birth Number**)

Note
Complete Workout Charts will be found in the back of this book. The little hearts will be used later for quick recognition.

Sometimes when you give people a reading they say 'But I'm not like that at all', and in a way they are quite right. There are reasons having to do with positive and negative readings (*pages 20–21*) and, as mentioned, Master Numbers (*page 22*), as will be explained later.

✦
Birth Number Charts

These are the read-outs for all Birth Numbers. The first section for each describes the more down-to-earth personality of the person; the second is soul-orientated. However, to me, all is one. We are here to learn and progress through the lessons the personality receives in life. These form and shape the spiritual self. All my read-outs will always be directed more towards the soul meanings than the 'earthly' ones.

Birth Number 1
Independent – Original – Creative – Pioneering

You should be well to the fore in anything you do, for yours is the number of the pioneer. 1s are born leaders, found where there is something original to do, things to be explored and creative action to be taken. Ambition and strong purpose figure in a 1's make-up – but they can be domineering so beware of getting other people's backs up and not understanding what you are doing that is so wrong.

In negativity, 1s dominating streak can be arrogant, selfish and downright inconsiderate, really too self-centred – never taking any mind of anybody else's problems.

In positivity, 1s can be relied on to be well-organized, efficient and a driving force in any undertaking – a very useful person to have around. They will never be afraid of anything new, in fact will revel in the chance to go out yonder to the latest wild frontier – be it physical, mental or spiritual.

Oddly, 1s have a dependent nature, especially in youth. They have to learn to leave this behind and seek the independence of '1 alone'. This is the life lesson for 1s: finding the ability to get on alone, then to reap the rewards of independence.

If the dependent state persists then you will be everybody's servant. Also it may be thought that self-centredness is independence. Independence lets others be themselves and demands nothing. Self-centredness doesn't give a hoot about others, and demands everything.

There is the possibility to accomplish so much that is worthwhile, either on your own or by working for, and with, others. Use your inner strength, your executive and administrative ability. The things to satisfy your undoubted needs will come to you by sheer force of your drive and ambition.

Spiritual Read-out on (the Governing Factor of) Birth Number 1

The governing factor of your spiritual life is that you are here to achieve independence. That is, to be able to cope alone and help and guide others less able by your fine example.

In your spiritual life you will tend towards the frontiers of esoteric thought. The 'way out' could more than interest you. Either you may find your own inner way to spirituality or be the leader in an organization already in existence. In both cases your ideas are unlikely to be closed-minded or staid.

Use your strong, warm personality to show the way to those of not quite so pioneering a nature, but remember your own need to experience individualization. Be your own person and do not slavishly follow another. This could happen if you manifest the negative of this factor, the tendency to be lazy. You can sidestep your responsibilities and even become dictatorial in manner. This latter is particularly not good in spiritual matters, where you should, as previously stated, lead by example.

This vibration will lead you to express yourself in interesting, even unusual ways, such as occult sciences, which may hold a great fascination for you. Your ideas, being particularly new and exciting, will interest others.

Sometimes this is a lonely number to bear in the life spiritual, but is nevertheless rewarding. It should never be dull but full of the excitement and wonder of often being the first to get there.

Birth Number 2
Balance – Understanding – Receptivity – Gentleness

Yours is the number of Partnership. 'Two by two' will, for you always work best with others rather than going it alone. This means you are better as part of a group or being the power behind the throne. You are wonderful at creating harmony because of your great sensitivity to others. But beware, this sensitivity is for yourself as well and can make you too timid in your dealings with others by over-reacting to people and situations.

In negativity, 2s can be moody and over-emotional. You are likely to love a gossip too well, being unable to keep a secret and perhaps betraying confidences.

In positivity, 2s have great consideration for others. They make a good friend to have, for they express their love and thereby gain its return.

2s make very strong bonds with others and within those bonds are usually the givers. Beware that others do not take advantage of this fact. You are the diplomats of this world and always know just the right thing to do or say in sticky situations. The love you give out freely oils the wheels of this world. You are unlikely to succeed in leadership for you do not have those kinds of strengths. Your success is often tied up with other people's, and your strength lies in support and helpfulness – all the good work you do behind the scenes. Be proud of this and you will find a great return of love and recognition.

An ability to deny oneself for the sake of others is a strong possibility with 2s; your lack of concern for material needs or status makes this possible. But you must not always stick to just a few people, get out there and get stuck in with larger groups. Learning to work as part of a team is a 2's life lesson, plus learning to cope with your sensitivity.

Spiritual Read-out on (the Governing Factor of) Birth Number 2

The governing factor of your spiritual life is the necessity to become a diplomat. 2 is the sign of partnership, and to make any partnership work at least one partner must be diplomatic in their dealings with the other. This will cultivate the silver tongue of the 2, which may then be used through life to ease many a difficult situation.

2s may spend much time waiting for tides to turn in their favour rather than being able to change them directly themselves. This teaches patience. Within the group or partnership the 2 will find their spiritual growth.

There can be a great deal of shyness here; with such a sensitive nature the 2 may withdraw from life. They may also appear to vacillate. Because others force change on 2s they can sometimes even practise deception to stop someone doing what 2 doesn't like or want. They must learn to stand up for themselves in group situations so they do not have to resort to such tactics which undermine their integrity.

Because 2 is a feminine principle of our dual nature, sometimes when they are hard-pressed to keep their equilibrium they must learn to reflect the opposite or masculine principle to keep their balance.

In past lives 2s may have ignored the needs of others; they will be brought face-to-face with this during their life under the 2 vibration.

Birth Number 3
Versatile – Energetic – Sociable – Artistic

Here we have the expression of joy! Or we should have, for 3s are here to learn the expression of self, usually by their artistic, creative abilities, or at the very least a love of beautiful things. You surround yourself with things of beauty, from warm friendships to the lovely objects for which your soul craves. Do not let this joy in beauty run away with you, making you light-hearted, superficial and frivolous.

In negativity, if you do not develop your undoubted capabilities you may draw back into yourself, hiding rather than expressing your feelings.

In positivity, you are very adaptable and able to take on a persona for any given moment. Your wide circle of friends recognize your versatility.

You are at your best using your voice for communicating. 3s are life's great actors, singers and salespeople, taking delight in expressing themselves. 3s sometimes spread their talent over too many areas and dissipate their worth. Find one or two things in which to become really expert. As a 3, be careful in entering business partnerships – you may find them restrictive.

3s are very observant, and bring their shrewdness to bear on any situation. This can bring success linked with an ability to work hard. You don't like taking orders, although you will, for a time. If giving orders you can become a mite dictatorial. Curb that outspokenness when dealing with slower mortals. Though not possessive or jealous, nobody takes advantage of you. 3s are fun to be with, full of wit and impulsively generous. But once you have done with a relationship, you have done with it for ever.

Spiritual Read-out on (the Governing Factor of) Birth Number 3

The governing factor of your spiritual life is that of expression of latent talents. One of the main spiritual lessons of this vibration is to remain in positive optimism and not descend into negative pessimism. Another is not to let the good things of life crowd out all thoughts of higher awareness.

Your 3 life will be busy and interesting, and you can slide through it in an easy-going manner enjoying the experience. However, you can form bad habits which are very hard to eradicate.

In all this 'joy of living' you must learn to distinguish the needs and desires of the lower, earthly self from those of the higher self.

Any consciousness of the spiritual that you do gain can be imparted to others by you better than most, for you should have a well-developed gift of communication. You can turn people's thoughts towards their own higher selves by beautiful pictures, sounds, or the voice used in any way. Or you could become a writer of plays or stories. Colour, form and sound are all yours to use to help others understand and awaken. Some will do this by making their home a place of beauty and harmony.

Do not use your endless energy on things of a wasteful nature, or waste your time chasing illusions. This negative side of your governing factor can be very strong and lead you to be intolerant of others' needs or ideas, and to become a gossip. This energy should be used only for constructive communication.

Birth Number 4
Calm – Efficient – Steady – Industrious

You should be the cornerstone of any enterprise, the builder, for 4s are to be relied on to master-mind, organize and work hard. You can be responsible and efficient, with a mathematical bent (4s are life's bookkeepers and accountants). Beware, though, as life can seem, or be, full of restrictions which hem you in on all sides. Learning to live with these restrictions is the lesson you have to learn.

In negativity, you can be weighed down with restrictions of all kinds – some of your own making because of your rather stubborn manner.

In positivity, you have a serious and honest approach to life. You are very conscientious and practical and easily know what is right and wrong.

Notwithstanding the fact that you have a difficult lesson to learn, you can be very successful because you are prepared to work hard. Your building abilities are much needed and respected. Your perseverance can see you through.

Build yourself a good base to work from – builders love a solid foundation on which to raise their house. This means making a good home life, which is very important to you, and being well trained so you know exactly what you are doing. But try not to let your attention to nitty-gritty details make you lose sight of the whole.

Frustration from restrictions placed on you can make you domineering and bossy. You sometimes wonder what the world has against you. Don't give up, 'When the going gets tough, the tough get going' and you are tough enough to cope. 4s are trustworthy, tenacious and most of all calm, they don't get upset easily. Remember others need your down-to-earth efficiency.

Spiritual Read-out on (the Governing Factor of) Birth Number 4

The governing factor of your spiritual life is that of will-power. This is developed by a life of practicality and, more unfortunately, by limitations that are put upon you in various ways during your life. Your spiritual evolvement will come by learning to use your will-power to overcome these limitations. You will be asked to take on responsibilities and exercise patience.

All this must be done in a cheerful way; no attempts to bemoan one's fate should be made. This is not an easy governing factor by any means, but nevertheless it can be most successful, for 4s pursue things right through to the end. They will build an organization which others are quite incapable of creating.

Care must be taken not to let will-power become the main factor in your dealings with others. This can quickly turn to domination to get one's own way. The leading you have to do must be by example if you want to grow and expand your own spiritual consciousness. Encourage tolerance within yourself.

This is the vibration of initiation, the ability to see things through and come out the other side a wiser, stronger person. You may prefer some form of religion or sect that has a strict set of rules rather than an easy-going one. This is fine as long as you don't make more of keeping to the letter of the law rather than its spirit. In other words, do not become narrow-minded or force others to accept only what you believe. There are many paths in the life spiritual; yours is not the only one.

Birth Number 5
Resourceful – Resilient – Adventurous – Clever

'Always on the move' is what is said about you. Freedom is what you are all about. You desire freedom from restrictions and plenty of new things to do. Travel, where you can experience change and variety, is great for 5s. Beware that you don't try so many things you get left with none and dissipate your chances by always wanting to go on to the next situation before the last is assimilated properly.

In negativity, a 5 can be afraid to use their freedom and retreat to some safe place, but there they will only suffer the frustration that any loss of freedom generates.

In positivity, you are very active – and versatility is your middle name. You have the ability to accomplish whatever you want to do. You have an ability to analyse.

What a bright one you are – 'bright-eyed and bushy-tailed' fits you to a 'T'. Always on the go, finding new things to do and ever ready to take a chance in life.

In fact, chance-taking may be taken to extremes. Your quick thinking leaves others breathless at times, so give them time to catch up.

You are able to take the stressful positions of life and not suffer too much, for you love the feeling of not knowing what is around the corner. Languages come easily to you – very useful in the life of a happy wanderer. Be careful not to get erratic, overdoing the change and adventure. What you are here to learn is constructive freedom. Freedom run riot can lead to over-indulgence in the delights of this world: sex, drink, drugs, eating too much, and so on. Seek a solid base from which to explore the world, somewhere to hang your hat for a while, it lends some stability. But if you leave a 'someone' there as well, remember they need your delightful companionship some of the time.

Spiritual Read-out on (the Governing Factor of) Birth Number 5

The governing factor of your spiritual life has the same connotation as the material reading, in that you have come, in this life, to learn constructive freedom. In the material life this may mean that you are someone who always wants to see and do new things. This continues in your spiritual wanderings, for you will have the ability to look over the entire scope of spiritual possibilities with enormous interest. It is doubtful if you will settle to any line of thinking that severely limited you. Any philosophy you take up needs to have many facets and give you lots to look at and ponder inwardly.

Indeed, when in your physical life you have been forced to remain in one place, the ability to roam the inward, metaphysical worlds gives you some peace and ability to cope.

This number connects with colour and sound. You should be able to work well within their sciences, which are linked with the new age of Aquarius. Take care that your spiritual self is not blanketed by the 5's propensity for illusion, that is, losing oneself in the illusion of material pleasures. Do not let bad habits become your master and stop your spiritual growth.

The 5 vibration should stir you to spiritual action and push you to search in the expanding levels of self-awareness which can lead to your overall growth. You will be given the opportunity to gain more experience than most, and this you gather on your travels around our wonderful world.

Birth Number 6
Harmonious – Loyal – Reliable – Honest

The home circle of relations and friends is most important to 6s, plus the responsibility this entails. But you love this responsibility and very rarely shirk it, gaining great happiness and pleasure from helping. But in always being willing to help almost anyone, beware, for they could take advantage of you. Learn to recognize those who really need your help.

In negativity, you may take on too much responsibility and become everybody's doormat. Turning away responsibility brings on feelings of guilt.

In positivity, you give out so much love and help it will come back to you sevenfold. You bring balance to your marriage and usually love children.

We all look to you for help and sympathy, and you are usually very willing to oblige. Material needs for yourself are not your top priority and you will often sacrifice for others what you have, and even what your family has. Best check if the family are willing before giving everything away.

Sometimes a confusion can arise in that you think 'responsibility' means 'dominating' any given situation. You can expect too much of others, and be fussy and critical. 6s are life's social workers, nurses and counsellors. Here they can use their sense of responsibility to great advantage.

6s can be very artistic and love to have and show off a beautiful home. They can quite often be musicians, painters and writers. Your lesson in this life is to show love and balance in responsibility, enjoying your loving circle of family and friends – you deserve them.

Spiritual Read-out on (the Governing Factor of) Birth Number 6

The governing factor of your spiritual life is that of the expression of love – a love that is unconditional, that requires no return. It is often expressed within a home circle but should be taken out further. In this life you are learning to align yourself with the creative force, which is love, and to develop this force within yourself.

In early years this may lead to seeking love of a physical nature and not understanding that it is really a cosmic love that should be sought. This can lead to some heartaches until you learn to love in a non-possessive way. Although you need returned love you must also learn to be independent of the need of it.

As a 6, going about your business you may find people will load you with responsibilities. As this is a part of your lesson you must shoulder them with willingness but not to the point that you become a doormat for all to use. Responsibility implies wisdom in accepting it.

Sometimes a 6 can get on the negative track of this vibration and love in a manner that is conditional or smothering for others. Check this tendency, as it is not leading you towards your goal of reflecting true love.

Something to watch out for is getting trapped in the small circle of home and immediate friends, so encourage yourself to get out and meet a wider group of people. Cosmic love is not to be limited but given to all, so that you begin to feel a part of all that is.

Birth Number 7
Contemplative – Mystical – Philosophical – Intellectual

'Different' is the word for 7s. You think and act differently, making it very hard for others to understand you – in fact, do you understand yourself? Even with all your introspective thinking, analysing and contemplation, it's odds on you don't. Lovely fey people, 7s, with a touch of the mysterious about them, as if viewing a world others cannot see – and that's just what they may be doing! You are likely to live in a world of your own making, but beware you don't completely lose touch with the everyday world.

In negativity, you can be distant, sarcastic and at times moody. At worst, a 7 can become completely dissociated from reality and rambling in speech.

In positivity, your deep search for wisdom can benefit all of humanity. Your relationships are very deep and meaningful. You are very intuitive, with perceptive qualities.

'How deep is the ocean?' Probably not deeper than a 7. Much time is taken up thinking, studying and making sense of the world about you. You are a grand dreamer of spectacular dreams, but usually not someone who will actually do something about them. You are not very adaptable, especially to the modern world, although you may make use of technology that is useful to your purposes. You like to spend a lot of time alone. 7s are the philosophers, poets and scholars of this life, not too worried about material gain. They can survive on very little.

Don't fear loneliness or failure or you will find life very difficult. Solitary as you are, you do need some recognition to function well, but learn to operate even if it does not come. You are on track if you are finding the deep truths of life, then offering them, with great humility, to others.

Spiritual Read-out on (the Governing Factor of) Birth Number 7

The governing factor of your spiritual life is that of inspiration. 7s are very sensitive and are often aware of higher consciousness without any suggestion from anybody else. They should seek that still small voice within, for from there will come all answers to their problems and, more importantly, inspiration of a higher nature. This can manifest as mediumistic qualities and, used in the right way, can lead to explanations of the universe which all humanity can share in.

This inner gift can also manifest by way of artistic creativeness such as painting, composing music or writing poetry. Any of these can lead others towards their inner self.

Great care must be taken within all this introspection not to be fooled by illusion. This may take the form of possessions, which come to mean too much to you. This is the lower end of this vibration and can lead to despondency, moodiness and criticism of others. There can also be a chance of thinking oneself better than the rest because of the revelations one might have received. Spiritual snobbery is just as bad as the material kind.

This wonderful vibration, used positively, can demonstrate higher awareness more than any other, for 7s are a link between heaven and earth.

7s nearly always have a purpose in coming to earth, but they can get lost in meditative grandeur and forget it. They may also be asked to make a great sacrifice somewhere in order to fulfil this purpose.

Birth Number 8
Tenacity – Concentration – Toughness – Drive

Yours is the number of the businessperson in this life; when you work hard you gain substantial material rewards. There are no grey areas here – you can fail just as wildly as you can succeed, though success is the more likely of the two. The pursuit of the material things in life will take up most of your time, but beware that once you have gained them you have to learn the lesson of how to enjoy them.

In negativity, 8s may chase power and wealth to the exclusion of all else. The temptations of misusing these may leave you facing hostile reactions.

In positivity, your self-confidence and ambition will nearly always bring success. You can reach dizzy heights in all you do.

Much satisfaction can be gained in the mastering of the outward world. No inward gazing for you, but practical, down-to-earth hard work. 8s can be the politicians of this life, as organizing on a grand scale is definitely their forte. 8s can fail when they are afraid to take the risks involved, and will then be very frustrated with their lives. This is unusual, for mostly they become kingpin in their chosen field and have their fair share of the good life. Care must be taken not to misuse these rewards. 8s are likely to be the bankers, lawyers and stockbrokers of the world – and among the very best of them too.

You make very loyal and stable partners, but can be physically rather undemonstrative. You often feel the material gifts you bring to your partner makes up for this, but don't judge everyone's needs by your own. Also remember it's the striving that should bring satisfaction, not the goal achieved.

Spiritual Read-out on (the Governing Factor of) Birth Number 8

The governing factor of your spiritual life is restraint. The 8 is looked upon as the number of material success and gain. 8s will often be in the forefront of the business world and work unbelievably long hard hours to gain their ends. It might be thought this is the number of 'luck', as wealth often comes their way. What is not realized is that this success is really a very hard lesson, for it is administered to help you find the inner, spiritual self and learn not to rush headlong into materiality. It is the lesson of recognizing the illusion of the material. The 8 will find many opportunities to fight the lower, egotistic self who thinks itself so clever at making all this money.

Years ago 8s might have run to hide within religious walls where materiality was at a minimum, so unable to tempt them. Today they must accept that their fight is out in the world, and of course, when they win, the gain is that much greater.

So use your abilities to lead the world. Many good causes need your acumen to acquire wealth, or within your business you can demonstrate the brotherhood of man. Leadership is what has to be developed, and we are in need of spiritual leadership more than any other.

Work hard and use your strong practical nature to get the best out of this world. Then realize that worldly glittering prizes are a sham compared to spiritual prizes. Use what you have gained to help the whole of humanity, or at least part of it.

Birth Number 9
Spiritual – Humanitarian – Courageous – Successful

'Wider still and wider' should your bounds be set! Broad-mindedness is what your life lesson is all about. This and using your gift of giving. You can give in your partnerships and friendships as well as in the wider scale of universal giving. Your happiness will be found in the act of giving, but beware not to spread yourself too thin among all the humanitarian pursuits that you would like to lend your ever-ready hand to help.

In negativity, 9s can feel that selflessness is not that satisfying. They may try to attain material goals – but will find them very disappointing.

In positivity, 9s find that service, understanding and compassion are unequalled. They will give and give of themselves for their weaker brethren in life.

You are better working for yourself than for others, but are likely to be happiest in organizations of a compassionate nature. 9s are often found in international aid organizations because of their ability to see the wider issues. They are very energetic, almost workaholics for worthwhile causes. They are fighters and capable of great mental achievement.

Regretfully, some 9s can be small-minded and prejudiced. Those who don't learn to give of themselves become intolerant and uncompassionate, but a true 9 is a lovely, broad-minded, far-seeing and helpful person. You see things through to the end and are often found tying up all the loose ends others forget. 9 is a difficult life lesson, as you seem to set off in the direction opposite the one you want in order to get to where you want to go. Also, oddly, you will find love, friendship and satisfaction when you give up the idea that you need these things. Then they will come to you in full.

Spiritual Read-out on (the Governing Factor of) Birth Number 9

The governing factor of your spiritual life is selfless service. 9s are the humanitarians of the world, or should be. On this vibration your spiritual life is enhanced by caring for the many needy. This must be done, in most cases, without reward. Of course, there are those who make it their profession by working for some organization, but even they must try to keep remuneration to a minimum. Your reward is gratitude for your ministrations. But best of all, for your personal growth, no reward is needed or expected.

This loving, selfless giving is the culmination of past life experience. Now you come to fulfilment and the end of a cycle in 9. The influence of the 9 vibration is to stimulate the desire to be of service to all. Healing, both physical and mental, is a gift that can very easily be in the make-up of a 9. The giving of spiritual and other counselling is a possibility. Beware of overdoing the good works to the detriment of your own health. It is quite possible to get carried away, and if your strength breaks down, nobody is helped.

Do not set in motion that which you cannot accomplish in this life, for, as previously stated, this is the end of a cycle. You should feel inwardly the task you have come specifically to do this lifetime. Try not to ignore the demands of giving which this number generates, for it will possibly rebound on you.

Note for Numerologist
If the Birth Number is 11, please note that sometimes people reject the hardships of a Master Number and revert to the single digit – in this case 2 (1 + 1 = 2). Point this out to the sitter and give them the reading for 2 as well as 11. They are more likely to accept the 2, as few can cope with a Master Number's demands. (*See details on page 22.*)

Birth Number 11
Illumination – Selflessness – Humanitarian – Giving

11 represents illumination. It is a number which should make one aware that there is more to life than what can be seen with the material eye. You should have a different kind of perception, and a different way of understanding, if you have taken the trouble to develop them. Beware these rather different faculties don't lead you into a world of fantasy, separating you from reality. 11s can suffer badly from nervous tension.

In negativity, don't get lost in your dream world. If you use your special powers to gain things for yourself you may accomplish much but still feel dissatisfied.

In positivity, 11s all have important things to do in this life which will help mankind progress, that's why they are here. They must use their undoubted skills and talents to bring about a better world.

11s, you must develop your inner forces and become aware of what you are and of your special knowledge, gained in many past lives. Then use your illumination for the benefit of everybody. The materiality of this world is not really for you, the spiritual should be uppermost.

Spiritual Read-out on (the Governing Factor of) Birth Number 11

The governing factor of your spiritual life is that of inspiration derived from illumination. This will lead you into many hard and testing situations, but you have the wherewithal to succeed using the illumination gained from your many previous lives. Growth made under this vibration is of the highest cosmic nature. So hard can this path be, it is not surprising many opt out – some by reverting to the single digit (2) and others by retreating into a world of illusion. Yet others join fanatical sects or religions, believing that their strict rules will keep in check the wonderful, yet terrifying, things that go on within themselves.

Those strong enough to grasp the opportunities of this vibration will bring great illumination to mankind. Unfortunately many of their schemes and ideas seem impractical to others, so care must be taken not to get caught up in idealistic talk but instead to produce very practical ideas which can be utilized and understood by more ordinary mortals.

Note for Numerologist
If the Birth Number is 22, please note that sometimes people reject the hardships of a Master Number and revert to the single digit – in this case 4 (2 + 2 = 4). Point this out to the sitter and give them the reading for 4 as well as 22. They are more likely to accept the 4, as few can cope with a Master Number's demands. (*See details on page 22.*)

Birth Number 22
Master Builder – Potential – Idealism – Power

22 is the Master Builder and should head any really large organization or be in a position of great power. But beware, from the ranks of the 22s can also come the 'mastermind' behind large and daring criminal activities.

In negativity, you can sometimes back off from your potential and powers. Then you accomplish very little and suffer from nervous tension.

In positivity, you are an extremely capable person and understand the innate forces at work in this world. You harness and use them with skill.

You will do best and realize the full potential of the Master Number if you start new movements or take over the running of those in existence. Preferably these should be altruistic and humanitarian – healing organizations, welfare centres or charities. Politics can also beckon.

There are not many 22s accomplishing all they could. Come on 22s, the world needs your abilities desperately!

Spiritual Read-out on (the Governing Factor of) Birth Number 22

The factor governing your spiritual life is that of being a Master Builder. This vibration is the culmination of the 22 vibration, where thoughts are turned into practical use in the highest way. Here you should be demonstrating the oneness of all things within creation, and also the power of spirit over matter.

This is one of the most difficult vibrations on which to succeed, and many opt out by reverting to their single digit number of 4 or going for material gain, which they are superbly fitted to do. They will feel frustrated in either case, for those with a Master Number have come to earth with a special mission and if they ignore it they will only have to come again to complete it. So why not look it in the face here and now? Deep inside you know what it is that you have to do. Whatever it is, it should leave a lasting mark on our world and benefit all.

Give yourself a time every day to look inwardly and find the answers. This will help you to have an insight as to what has to be done. This is a difficult vibration spiritually, demanding so much as it does, so stay positive and balanced.

The Positive and Negative Numbers

How could a meaning be wrong, yet right? If you look at the list of meanings given for each birth number again you will notice that most of them are fairly 'positive' in outlook: Leadership, Communication, Balance, Material Success, Generous and so on. What would be the opposite? Timidity, Uncommunicative, Unbalanced, Material Failure, Meanness. These opposites are referred to as 'negative'.

If you take an emotion such as Love and imagine it to be the positive end of a stick, then the other end would be the negative Hate. But it is all one stick; either end may be expressed, and any mixture of both along the length of the stick. If the stick were a see-saw with a central pivot, you could imagine it being balanced in the middle: neither too loving nor too hateful. But if one end were to touch the ground, then the balance could be said to have come down more strongly on one side than the other.

So when dealing with a subject whose numbers *say* they should be a Home-loving 6, and they come to have a reading with a back-pack and say they have never slept under the same roof for two nights in a row, then they are obviously expressing the Negative of 6. If their number is a Freedom-loving 5 and they have locked themselves away in some job where they never even see the light of day, then it is equally obvious they are expressing the Negative of 5.

Getting this idea of Positive AND Negative is very important in numerology. Most of us start out expressing the negative in our early lives; during our lifetime we work and move towards expressing the positive. For example, we may go from the shy negative of 3 to the socially interactive person that is a true 3, or from unintuitive, non-mystical 7 to the 7 deeply into mysticism and wildly intuitive, or from the thoughtless negative of 9 to the expansive humanitarian positive of 9.

So let's look at another list, this time charting the negative meanings of the numbers:

1   Conventionalist, Follower, Needy of others, Selfish

2   Alone, Power on the Throne, Undiplomatic, Insensitive

3   Uncommunicative, Miserable, Inexpressive, Asocial

4   Lazy, Failure due to Limitations, Disordered

5   Enslaved, Staying Put, Aimless

6   Hate, Having No Family, Imbalanced, Taking No Responsibility

7   Non-psychic, Materialist, Non-analytical, Conventional

8   Material Failure, Unbusinesslike, Not Materially Minded

9   Self-seeking, Mean, Uncooperative, Conventional in ideas

11 & 22   See below

Do not be black-and-white with these meanings. If someone expresses hate it does not mean they cannot love. If someone is helpful at times it does not mean they are not, at other times, unhelpful. These meanings are *tendencies*. As we progress through life we may be at any point along the balance of the see-saw. Some get to the end of their lives still expressing the Negative. Others are born expressing the Positive and never go on to express the Negative. But then, very few of us are these saints!

✶
Master Numbers 11 and 22

With 11s and 22s it is not so much a matter of their meanings having a Negative, rather that for some reason there is a failure to express the true meaning of 11 or 22. This needs some deeper explanation.

Master Numbers are higher vibrations, stronger energies. They are difficult to cope with and it takes an experienced person to undertake a life expressing these stronger traits. Sometimes they find that they just cannot manage it, the effort is too much. So they fall back to their lower number. For the 11 this is 2 (1 + 1 = 2) and for the 22 this is 4 (2 + 2 = 4). I call this Backing Off into the lower number. So the Negative of 11 and 22 is to Back Off into the easier expressions of 2 and 4.

If you or your subject have the Master Number of 11 or 22, then you must also look carefully at the 2 and 4 meanings to see if they apply. Often you will find that the person expresses both. They may swing between the two, depending on how they are coping with the energies. This makes them quite complicated people and they almost invariably suffer from nervous tension.

Now here we have the kind of discovery which numerology can point up and shed much-needed light on. 11s and 22s may have suffered greatly from this nervous tension and not understood why. When the swing from one number to the other is explained, usually they will readily understand – after all they do have Master Numbers and they will try to do something to alleviate their problems. Always try to encourage them to express the higher vibration, for they will surely have come into this life to be of great use to humanity.

The Numbers of Our Names

Birth Numbers are relatively simple to work out. Although this is a most important number, it only gives us the meanings of our life path, the basic sort of person we are likely to be, and the basic lessons we have come to learn. Let us plunge into some really interesting work and discover how we express the Birth Number, what our Soul Urge is, and the deep inner wish I call 'The Twist in the Tail'.

First we have to turn the letters of the alphabet into numbers. I have used the usual Western method of allocating these numbers, namely:

1	2	3	4	5	6	7	8	9
A	B	C	D	E	F	G	H	I
J	K	L	M	N	O	P	Q	R
S	T	U	V	W	X	Y	Z	

In other words, the letters of the alphabet are assigned the numbers 1 - 9, then 1 - 9 again, and then 1 - 8. It is an extremely simple code to remember and, with use, you will find it is soon committed to memory. If not, I suggest that you make a copy of this chart to keep with you.

Now we must consider the name of our subject. There are a few rules to follow here, which are invariable:

1 The name used is the one the person was given at birth and was christened with or registered as on their birth certificate.

2 If the person was adopted before the age of 6 months, then the surname used is that of the adoptive parents, for this is the name the subject came to experience.

3 For married women use the née or maiden name (as in 1. and 2. above), *not* the married name.

4 Never use any nickname, changed or shortened name in any circumstances.

5 It is suggested that only the first of any middle names is used. This is usually sufficient. Any more makes for a long and difficult reading, especially if the person has been named after the players of an entire football team!

✳

When a Name Changes

Here I must discuss the matter of change of name and names generally. You will find many people say such things as 'But I never use that name' or 'I have *never* been called by that name,' or other such comments. Ignore all their protestations and stick to your guns, USE ONLY THE NAMES AS GIVEN AT BIRTH. It is essential. I cannot stress this enough. Do remember this particularly for your own reading.

If I may, I will illustrate this for you. I was invited to appear on a local radio programme and I asked for the programme presenter's details to do a reading for him. He had changed his name for career purposes, as many do, and was not very willing to give me his original name. I persisted and offered confidentiality as to the original name, which he then gave me. On doing his 'chart', another way of saying a reading, I discovered that the original name was made up of three 3s – thus his expression, soul urge and twist in the tail all said COMMUNICATION! How well he had chosen his career. What else would have suited him better? The new name, although a very nice name and quite suitable for a radio personality, had nothing much numerologically in support of his chosen career.

It was this man's original name that gave him his energies. Had I done the chart on his 'stage name' it would have appeared that he had chosen entirely the wrong life path for himself. So put aside any reasons, protestations or doubts and insist on the original name, abiding by the rules above. Do not do a reading for anyone not willing to give or use his or her original name.

Believe it or not, you chose your name and it was thought out very carefully to give you the right energies, bring you the right lessons and give you a chance to work things out. You may not agree with this, but let me ask you to try to accept it for the time being and make your mind up later, after you have experienced more practical numerology.

But what about changed names? Women marrying have always, until very recently, had to take another name. Does it have any effect? Yes, it does, but it is minor compared to the energies of the original name. I put it like this – if you imagine that the original name is a sculpted figure, clearly visible, and then the new or changed name is a fine veil thrown over the statue, you can still see the figure underneath but it is not so clear.

So a changed name may cloud the original energies or even divert them a little, but not entirely change them. In some schools of numerological thought it is felt that a new name will bring about a change, better luck and so on. I do not subscribe to this idea. If you have gone to all the effort to experience the particular energies, lessons, etc. that your name gives you, then I suggest that you take the chance to do just that. Oddly, even before I knew anything about numerology I always preferred to address people, where possible, by their full name, not a shortened version. Perhaps I was intuitively realizing this point when I did so.

So lets get to the actual reduction of a name.

Finding the Numbers in a Name

We will return to John and Jane and work on their full names.

John's full name is John Damian Fullerton. We now have to numerize the name using our alphabet block (*see page 23*). So we get:

JOHN DAMIAN FULLERTON
1 6 8 5 4 1 4 9 1 5 6 3 3 3 5 9 2 6 5

In this way we have found the numbers of his name. Some numerologists do add these numbers straight across, but I prefer the method set out below, which offers deeper meanings.

The letters of a name consist of consonants and vowels; you will remember the A, E, I, O, U of school days, no doubt, all other letters being consonants. We use this in numerology to break up the name. Thus we can have the alphabet block set out in a straight line, with vowel numbers above and consonants below.

1   5   9   6   3 5 7

A B C D E F G H I J K L M N O P Q R S T U V W X Y Z

2 3 4 6 7 8 1 2 3 4 5 7 8 9 1 2 4 5 6 7 8

No, I have *not* made a mistake: W and Y are sometimes vowels and sometimes consonants. This is a legacy of our mixed language sources. Sometimes our W is pronounced as in *wolf*, and sometimes as in *flow* (an *oou* sound, as the name DOUBLE U suggests). Sometimes the Y is as in *Yes*, sometimes the *iee* of Lady. There are other sounds for these two letters as well. So basically the rule comes down to this:

If the W or Y comes immediately after a vowel, or where there is no (other) vowel in the syllable, or where it sounds like a vowel, then the W or Y is numbered as a vowel.

So in BETTY the Y is a vowel –

in RAWLEY both the W and the Y are vowels –

in WANDA the W is a consonant –

in YOLANDA the Y is a consonant

and so on.

I test it by pronouncing the name. If it sounds like a vowel or stands for a vowel in the absence of a true vowel for the sound – then it is a vowel. Anything else and it's a consonant.

Some numerologists do not use this rule and so will arrive at different numbers for the name. I have found, after doing hundreds of charts for people, that this method gives the truer reading, particularly for what I call Soul Readings. I therefore advise you to take the little extra trouble to get a correct reading.

Now we take John's name and set it out like this:

```
    6      1 91    3   5   6
 J O H N  D A M I A N  F U L L E R T O N
    1    8 5 4    4    5 6 3 3 9 2 5
```

We could now add up the numbers straight across, but as I expect you will have guessed, if we do this we will miss some other useful numbers. So we add each name separately, moving our calculations up for vowels and down for consonants, as shown in Figure 1.

```
       …6……………        +…………11……………+ ………5……………
  ↑…6 …………… /…………11 (not added) / ………14 (add 1+4).
  ↑…6 …………… /………1+…..9+1……… / ….3+……5+…….6….
Name↓↑J O H N     / D A M I A N   /F U L L E R T O N
  ↓  1+…8 + 5……… /….4 +….4+…….+5…./. 6+…3 + 3..+..9 + 2 +…5.
  ↓  14 (add 1+4)…… /….13…… (add 1+3)…../ .28…(add 2+8)……….
  ↓  5……………… /….4………………… / .10 …(add 1+0)……….
     5……………… +….4………………… + .1…………………………
```

Figure 1

You notice that we stick to the rule of not reducing Master Numbers, so the number of the name DAMIAN is an 11.

We now take each reduced vowel or consonant number from each name, that is, the top and bottom lines of our chart, and add them up. Thus:

Top Line (Vowels): 6 + 11 + 5 = 22 = John's Vowel Number

Bottom Line (Consonants): 5 + 4 + 1 = 10 (1 + 0) = 1 = John's Consonant Number.

Figure 2 shows a Name Workout Chart with John's name and numbers laid in:

Vowel Number ⇓

```
    …6……………    +…………11……………+ ………5……………… =«22»/22
    …6 ……………    /…………11(not added)/ ………14(so add1+4)…↑….
    …6 ……………    /………1+….9+1…….  / ……3+……5+…….6…..↑….
Name J O H N       /  D A M I A N    /F U L L E R T O N ↑
    1+…8+5………    /…..4+….4+……..5…. /.6+…3+3..+.9+2+…5. ↓
    14(so add1+4)  /….13(so add1+3)…… / …28(so add2+8)…… ↓
    5………………    /……..4………………  / …10(so add1+0)……. ↓
    5………………    +……..4………………  + …1…………………….=«10»/1..↓
```

Consonant Number ⇑..↓

Add **Vowel** & **Consonant Numbers** between «.» together and reduce «.32»/◆ ……5

Whole Name Number ⇑

………………/……………… **Given Names Totals**

Add the **Vowel** & **Consonant Numbers** of each name separately and write them in the space above

Figure 2

Please Note

I will now dispense with adding any zero numbers like 10, 20 etc. and will go straight to the final number – 1, 2, etc. Zero is only used in one instance in this book as a Numerological number (*see page 89*).

Did you see the last line at the bottom of Figure 2, where it says 'Given Name Totals'? Here you add the final number of the vowels and consonants of each Given Name together – that is, 6 and 5 for John, 11 and 4 for Damian, and place the results on the line directly below the name. These calculations will be used later; ignore them for the time being.

This method may seem cumbersome and long-winded, but it gains certain numbers either not obtained by other methods, or different numbers which

I have found are more correct for the subject. For instance, you may think somebody has a Master Number and they haven't, until this method reveals one in one of their names.

May I particularly point out to you the fact that for the Whole Name Number you add up the first single number (or double number, if that's what it is) arrived at on both the vowel and consonant lines – that is, those between the «…» signs (22 and 10 for John) – to find the first number for the Whole Name Number, which has a (beside it (in John's case, 32, which becomes 5). As mentioned, this could be a single or double number which you reduce in the normal way.

In the same way that we wrote John's Birth Number 13/4, we now write John's Whole Name Number as 32/5. His Vowel Number is 22/22, his Consonant Number 10/1. The second number is the one we use to discover the meanings of his Birth and Whole Name Numbers.

Sometimes the numbers do not add up to a double number. Say the three vowels are 1, 3, 2 – making a total of 6. In this case the Vowel Number would be written as 6/6, with the first 6 used to discover the Whole Name Number. This can happen with the Whole Name Number and/or the Birth Number.

But first let's work out Jane's full name for practice (Figure 3). Her full name is Jane Rose Kirkby.

Name Chart   **Vowel Number**   ⇓

......6...........	+............11...........	+	.............7...........	=«24» / 6
.....6...........	/............11...........	/	..........16.............	↑....
...1..+..5........	/............6..+..5........	/	.........9....+......7........	↑....

Name   J A N E   /   R O S E   /   K I R K B Y   ↑

1 ....+...5........	/.........9....+..1...........	/	......2..+..9+2+2..........	↓
.......6...........	/............10.............	/	.............15...........	↓
......6...........	/.............1.............	/	............6................	↓
......6...........	+.............1.............	+	............6................	↓=«13» / 4 ↓

Consonant Number ⇑..↓

Add **Vowel** & **Consonant Numbers** between «..» together and reduce«..37» /◆ 10/1

Whole Name Number   ⇑

......12/3......../......12/3........ **Given Names Totals**

Add the **Vowel** & **Consonant Numbers** of each name separately and write them in the space above

Figure 3

So Jane has a

- Birth Number 15/6
- Vowel Number 24/6
- Consonant Number 13/4
- Whole Name Number 10/1

In some cases the Whole Name Number may be large and have to be reduced twice or even three times, as in 66 (6 + 6 = 12, then 1 + 2 = 3).

Now work out your own name numbers using the blank Workout Chart (Figure 4) below. Then practise working out the name numbers for various friends and relations. You can photocopy the Workout Chart to help in this task. When you have done several to use as examples, then carry on with the next section, where we will begin to read and understand their meanings.

Additional blank Workout Charts will be found at the back of this book.

Name Chart   **Vowel Number** ⇓

```
................... +.......................... +........................... =«..»/..
................... /.......................... / ...........................↑....
................... /.......................... / ...........................↑....
Name    _____/_____/_____  ↑
................... /.......................... / ...........................↓
................... /.......................... / ...........................↓
................... /.......................... / ...........................↓
................... +.......................... +........................... ↓=«..»/..↓
```

                               Consonant Number ⇑..↓

Add **Vowel** & **Consonant Numbers** between «..» together and reduce «...» /◆ .....

                                    Whole Name Number ⇑

................./................... **Given Names Totals**

Add the **Vowel** & **Consonant Numbers** of each name separately and write them in the space above

Figure 4

'Transformers'

Putting Together the Birth Number, Whole Name Number, Vowel and Consonant Numbers

We now have four numbers which we can use to discover the soul readings for John and Jane: the Birth Number, the Whole Name Number, the Vowel Number and the Consonant Number. The first three are the most important, while the fourth, the Consonant Number, is only a minor vibration to consider.

The Birth Number is the basic number on which all else hinges. It is the colour of the self in this incarnation. A soul comes to experience the particular energy or vibration and the lessons that the number gives – to be individual (1), to learn to communicate (3) to be a businessperson and experience materiality (8), and so on.

If this were the only number to consider, then we would have a very dull world with only the basic 9 personalities plus some Master Numbers. This is obviously not so. We are so diverse that it is impossible to find two people alike in every way. Some come close, as with twins, who usually have the same number (unless one is born before midnight and the other after), but there are always differences. This difference lies in the Name Number, which *transforms* the basic Birth Number.

To use an analogy, if you have two glasses of water into which you pour blue dye in equal amounts, you have two glasses of blue water. If you then pour a little yellow dye into one and red into the other, what you have is one glass of green water and one of mauve. Yet both were blue to start with. The second colour has *transformed* the first. If we then went on putting in small amounts of various colours, each glass of water would be further transformed until each its own totally individual colour. But the original blue is still there, doing its work to make up the final colour.

This is how I see numerology. The Birth Number is the original colour, and all the others transform or change it a little bit, some more than others.

Numerology helps us to see all the colours we have within us, that affect us and make us who and what we are.

The most important transformer is the Whole Name Number. This number shows how the Birth Number will be expressed. John's Birth Number of 4 (hard work, orderliness, etc.) will be expressed by his Whole Name Number of 5 (constructive freedom). Jane's Birth Number of 6 (Love, Balance, etc.) will be expressed by her Whole Name Number of 1 (individuality).

John's 4 is transformed by the vibration of 5, so that he may fight with himself to decide whether to stay put in an ordered existence or strike out to see what is over the hill, throwing all caution to the winds. Jane, poor soul, has to live with a conflict going on internally of wanting to be a homemaker extraordinaire, blending and being in balance with everybody, yet at the same time expressing it so individually that it could put people's backs up.

On a more upbeat note, John might use the 5 to break out of the limitations that 4 brings, and Jane might set about homemaking in an original and individual new way which brings benefit to all, say as an interior designer.

Remember, the Birth Number is the most important and gives the traits most likely to be encountered in the person whose chart you are doing. The Whole Name Number then tells you how it is expressed. A 7 with a 3 wants to communicate all the inner searchings he or she has been conducting. An 8 with a 9 might want to give all their hard-earned goods away.

The charts in this book will provide a fair read-out, but it is your task as you progress with numerology to realize and explain the different transformers affecting the person having his or her reading done. It will be your syntheses which will bring out the individual energies and how they affect one another.

So here are the Whole Name Number charts, which are again divided into sections: first the worldly read-out, then the spiritual.

Whole Name Number Charts

Whole Name Number 1

Self-reliance is what your potential is all about. You must learn to talk in the singular whenever possible, for you are here to develop the 'self', the I. This does not mean doing this in a selfish manner, but to husband your inner resources and become a leader.

You have a very original approach to everything and can be creative in your ideas. But you might not always be the one to follow them through. Use your fine mind to achieve your ambitions in business, where you would really be best running your own. Don't become totally self-absorbed, nor bossy with others. Be the ambitious, positive, determined and self-confident person you are and you will fulfil your mission or destiny: *to show leadership.*

The Outer Expression of the Spiritual Self for 1

You will manifest your expression mainly through individualization of self and constructive leadership. The latter will be done mostly by personal example, but also you must show much patience with those who work under your direction. They may not always be able to see quite so clearly to the end of the road and its conclusions. If you misuse your authority in spiritual matters you will be in for more than a rude awakening.

The 1 vibration will often put you on some outpost of spirituality, for it is the number of the pioneer. There are more ways to be pioneered in the inner, spiritual life than out in the physical world. Your expression is to light the path for others.

Whole Name Number 2

Partnership is what your potential is all about. You must learn to develop your sympathy and understanding, for it will be sorely needed as you progress towards your role of being the peacemaker in many situations.

Partnership does not always mean just 'two' but can mean co-operating in a group. Here your inner resources will fit you for the job of diplomat, but be careful this ability doesn't land you with the job of mediating some difficult situations – however, if it does, yours are the best kid gloves going.

Be the courteous, considerate, tactful and friendly person you are and you will be well on the way to fulfilling your mission or destiny in life: *to be one of the peacemakers of this world.*

The Outer Expression of the Spiritual Self for 2

You will manifest your expression mainly through creating harmony amongst those who share your life. Yours is to work behind the scenes rather than in the full glare of the spotlight. Most of your spiritual work will be in group situations rather than alone. Here you will be loved, if not noticed, for the effort quietly put into everything. Your deeply sensitive nature tends to make you hide your light under a bushel, but others find it when in trouble and they seek your loving help.

Try to look at life with detachment, or your rather emotional reaction to things may do you harm. When you help others do not get personally involved or you may regret it. Just go on creating much-needed harmony everywhere.

Whole Name Number 3

Communication is what your potential is all about. You must learn to communicate your 'joie de vivre', joy of life, for you are here to cheer us all up. This does not mean being trivial or becoming a clown, but just using your ability to show us what a wonderful world we all live in.

Don't try to play at life or dissipate your forces; your inability to organize yourself leads you to waste your precious time. Think of one thing at a time and finish it. Don't flit from one thing to another quite so much. Sure, light-heartedness is very charming – but we all have to be serious at times.

Be the cheerful, happy, charming, gracious and loving person you are and you will fulfil your mission or destiny: *to inspire and uplift all you meet.*

The Outer Expression of the Spiritual Self for 3

You will manifest your expression mainly through self-expression. You should take all opportunities to learn to express your ideas and feelings, by any form possible. More than probably this will be in words, either spoken or written. It can be on a one-to-one basis or to larger groups.

The 3 brings a light-hearted air to life; you can express joy in living but you must watch that it does not become too frivolous. The things you are learning from your complete nature are important and must be communicated to others. What good will it be if you discover important facts that help the world if you don't get out there and tell everyone?

Whole Name Number 4

Service and order are what your potential is all about. You must learn to be totally organized, knowing where to put your hand on anything at any time. Show your reliability and steadfastness, then others will have confidence in you.

Don't let yourself get bossy and domineering – you can do this when you are frustrated by limitations put upon your organizational abilities: not enough money, resources, workers and so on. You have to learn to succeed despite these things, and you can, for you are persevering and determined.

By working long and hard and using your practical, down-to-earth qualities, all will be well. Be the systematic, helpful, honest, sincere person you are and you will fulfil your mission and destiny: *to build something really worthwhile.*

The Outer Expression of the Spiritual Self for 4

You will manifest your expression mainly through will-power. This does not mean dominating every person or situation, which is rather negative, but in the positive sense of the divine will. 'Not my will but thy will.' There will be a practical approach to things spiritual with this expression. 4 is the number of the builder, and you will help to build up any organization to which you give your allegiance. It will probably be of a conventional nature rather than something too far out.

Try not to hoard personal possessions or money. They will only keep you attached to the physical plane rather than letting you ascend to the higher planes of thought. Don't forget, rest is as important as work – make sure you get some.

Whole Name Number 5

Change and adaptability are what your potential is all about. You must learn to have and try out new ideas. You have the ability to catch on fast to any new ideas and put them to good use. You have to find out how to then present these some-times rather way-out ideas to other people – but then you should be good at selling anything, from new ideas to old fogies, to refrigerators to Eskimos.

Stick at it, don't get restless or impatient too soon. Your sometimes erratic behaviour is not easily understood by others. Watch out for any likelihood of over-indulgence in the good things of life. Be the enthusiastic, delightful, companionable and progressive person you are and you will fulfil your mission and destiny: *to help the world to adapt and change.* Something it is going to have to do if it is to survive.

The Outer Expression of the Spiritual Self for 5

You will manifest your expression mainly through the promotion of constructive freedom. This means communication of any kind, in order to tell people about the life spiritual. You should never be at a loss for words of encouragement and hope. This expression can be through any artistic medium or through sound. It will mostly be by voice, as 5s are renowned for being able to get an idea over to others.

So with the information you pick up in your spiritual wanderings, do not forget to make time to impart your findings to other souls. The expression of constructive freedom also means knowing what to do with freedom and using it in a worthwhile way. Be careful that this freedom is not of an escapist nature – that is, losing yourself in the illusions of pleasure.

Whole Name Number 6

Responsibility is what your potential is all about. You must learn to be a home-loving person and work to give your family a lovely place to live. When hosting, you make your guests comfortable and happy. Also you can show others the beauties of this world by example. These can be material, great works of design and art, or on the higher level of qualities of spirit.

Don't sacrifice yourself completely to the family or welfare of others. You have to learn where to draw the line. You could end up the family drudge.

Your love and concern for everyone and everything should be tempered with balance. Be the sympathetic, generous, kind, friendly and loving person you are and you will fulfil your mission and destiny: *to teach love of beauty and good taste to the world.*

The Outer Expression of the Spiritual Self for 6

You will manifest your expression mainly through love, responsibility and the home. This does not mean restriction, for love is the most pervasive of all expressions. Indeed, people on this vibration should have taken on board the ideal of universal brotherhood and will demonstrate that love is not a possessive – and therefore destructive – emotion. You will also feel for the under-dogs of this world and rush to their defence. This can lead to confrontations with authority.

Create harmony, beauty and comfort for all. Use your artistic talents to express your spirituality. Make a healing atmosphere around you, that all who come within your circle of acquaintance may benefit.

Whole Name Number 7

Mind power and observation are what your potential is all about. You must learn not to feel isolated when you are alone. You have a lot of studying and analysing to do to use your potential, which is about being able to distinguish falsehoods from truth, find out about the secret mysteries of this world, observe and think about all you see and feel, and find the silence of the inner self.

After this you must be able to pass on to others all the wisdom you have accumulated so they may benefit from it. Don't become so involved in heavenly things that you are no earthly good. Keep your two feet on the ground while your head is in those clouds. Be the rational, logical, interested person you are and you will fulfil your mission and destiny: *to use your well-developed mental powers to benefit others.*

The Outer Expression of the Spiritual Self for 7

You will manifest your expression mainly through intuition and inspiration. You can become a spiritual guide to others by using your natural sixth sense. You can also be a connection between heaven and earth, to bring to others the inspiration of the highest realms of light. If this expression causes you fear, then go in for more worldly counselling of others in the science of psychiatry or one of the many organizations such as those that deal with marriage counselling, the work done by the Samaritans, and so on.

Connect with the natural world as much as possible, as it will help you find the peace and quiet you need to think deeply about this world and the next. Don't let your sensitive nature spoil your life; it is hard knowing so easily what others are thinking, but that is your lesson for this life.

Whole Name Number 8

Self-discipline and mastery of self are what your potential is all about. You have to learn to work really hard, never give up when things look bleak, and achieve success by dint of your own efforts. Your potential is to be business-orientated, capable of running your own show, be it large or small. If you learn judgement of money situations, you could handle large sums of money with flair and ease. Character assessment could come just as easily to you.

Don't become materialistic to the exclusion of all else, or you will cut yourself off from everyone. Being intolerant or over-exacting may bring strain to relationships.

Be the efficient, organized, ambitious, energetic, self-confident and dependable person you are and you will fulfil your mission and destiny: *to demonstrate to the world how to deal with wealth and success correctly.*

The Outer Expression of the Spiritual Self for 8

You will manifest your expression mainly through coming to terms with power, money and restrictions. This may seem highly unspiritual, but you have to learn that the first two of these things are worldly illusions. You also have to learn how to retain thoughts of higher things while seemingly lost in materiality. Try to use your gains to benefit others.

Any restrictions are put in place to teach you personally to seek beyond wealth and power – otherwise there would be no pin-pricks in your seemingly easy life. Some people think this expression just means being very lucky, but they don't understand the lesson behind the acquisition of wealth and power. Use this expression to grow and learn many lessons vital for your future lives.

Whole Name Number 9

Selflessness and humanitarianism are what your potential is all about. You must learn temperance, forgiveness and sacrifice, and be ready to take anything the world can throw at you. You also have to develop the philanthropic touch and the potential to inspire others by your own works and deeds.

If you turn your back on this difficult potential, by lack of involvement, you can be self-centred, selfish, insensitive and unaware of others' needs and feelings. You can acquire an aloof attitude which makes it difficult for other people to love you, when that is what you really want. Be the idealistic, compassionate, tolerant, broad-minded, loving and generous person you are and you will fulfil your mission and destiny: *to inspire others by the ideal life you lead.*

The Outer Expression of the Spiritual Self for 9

You will manifest your expression mainly through humanitarianism. Some people call this 'do-gooding', but they have not realized the opportunities for spiritual advancement that comes through this lovely vibration of selfless giving.

So go ahead and love the world; it needs all your help and attention. Let love flow out from you so that others may see the joy of giving and follow your example.

A word of warning, though. 9s can have a highly volatile temperament; you must learn to control it at all times. You must also learn not to give and give until you are drained. This does no good at all. Conserve your energies for the most important work – there certainly is plenty out there for you to do.

Note for Numerologist

If the Whole Name Number is 11, please note that sometimes people reject the hardships of a Master Number and revert to the single digit of 2 (1 + 1). Point this out to the sitter and give them the reading for 2 as well as 11. They are more likely to accept the 2, as few can cope with a Master Number's demands.

Whole Name Number 11

Illumination and inspiration are what your potential is all about. You must learn to accept your destiny, to lead in public with good grace and live up to high standards. You have to promote better standards of life for everyone – and you can do this, for you have an inner understanding of spiritual and physical needs. This is because you can operate on psychic levels, which brings you a greater understanding of the world.

Don't let the likelihood of nervous tension spoil your life. You can dream too much and do too little. If you let fantasy win over fact you are on to a loser. This is a Master Number and more is expected of you. Don't worry, you have inner strength. Be the idealistic, deeply concerned, aware and sensitive person you are and you will fulfil your mission and destiny: *to be of selfless service to humanity.*

The Outer Expression of the Spiritual Self for 11

You will manifest your expression mainly through being a visionary. It is your path to care about others in all forms, from being a prison visitor to listening to spiritual problems in large or small numbers. You have to express humanitarianism. Admittedly this is usually in some organization of size for, after all, yours is a Master Number.

Unfortunately, those on this vibration can seem unrealistic in their ideas, and even thought peculiar by others. Develop practicality in the way you put over your ideas and you may have a better chance of their being accepted. Don't bury yourself in illusion and complexity. Simplicity in things spiritual is always better understood. To fulfil your destiny: *let your illumination shine forth.*

Note for Numerologist
If the Whole Name Number is 22, please note that sometimes people reject the hardships of a Master Number and revert to the single digit of 4 (2 + 2). Point this out to the sitter and give them the reading for 4 as well as 22. They are more likely to accept the 4, as few can cope with a Master Number's demands.

Whole Name Number 22

Power with responsibility is what your potential is all about. You must learn to accept great responsibility, be confident in your decision-making and serve the community with complete honesty and great love. This is quite a lot to live up to, but yours is a Master Number, the number of the master builder. You may be called upon to take charge of immense undertakings which benefit everyone.

Watch out that nervous tension does not spoil things. Turn away from your destiny and you can be selfish and dominating. Never, never be tempted to misuse your position of power or act in a dishonest manner. You have a potential invested with great trust.

Be the extremely capable, accomplished, perceptive, aware person you are and you will fulfil your destiny: *to bring to fruition large projects for the benefit of all.*

The Outer Expression of the Spiritual Self for 22

You will manifest your expression mainly through being a master builder. This Master Number is one of the hardest expressions to manifest, for you must try to create something of great worth. However, you have all your many past lives to draw on, and with hard work it can be accomplished. Here you have to combine the spiritual and intuitive with the material. You must manifest heaven on earth to make all who see your work think of their spiritual home – a very tall order indeed. You may come by great power and money in pursuing this aim, but you must remember this has to be returned in the form of good works. Your reward, if one is needed, is to be remembered long after you have left this world behind.

✴

Vowel Number

This is the third-most important Transformer. It could be called the Soul's direct input. We are incarnate in a body which has a personality. This is formed by our genetic background and our home life. Those into spiritual ideas also feel there is a further factor at work: our previous lives. Numerology is also of this latter opinion. This factor answers so many questions such as how twin brothers with identical backgrounds and genetic make-up can have totally different personalities. It is the input of previous personalities' experiences in former lives that can make all the difference.

As we have already discussed, our personality is expressed in different ways, as reflected in our Whole Name Number. The Vowel Number is the deep, inner divine self or soul, bringing its own vibration to bear on the personality incarnate in a body. I personally look at the Soul as the Divine life-giving spark that is within us all. It is this which progresses through all the spheres gathering experiences and learning about love. On its journey it takes various forms, personalities or series of personalities which, as they finish, go to make up the total soul.

In numerology it is felt that humans go through a series of incarnations; at the end of them all we will be ready to use all the knowledge we have gained in the service of the Soul. So the Soul, being this repository of our past experiences, and being in a position to know the future, can blend its total self into our present life via the Soul vibration found in the Vowel Number. It will push forward that which it knows is needed to round out this particular incarnation, or bring lessons needed by the whole.

Here are the readings for the Vowel Number, which although definitely relating to the spiritual still have an earthly reading as well as one designated as spiritual purpose.

✳
Vowel Number Charts

Vowel Number 1

You prefer to be free to be yourself, to act on your own. You are likely to be the leader in all you do, for this is the strong character trait you have brought with you from other lives. You are likely to dominate any given situation, but you are beginning to see the possibilities of higher consciousness rather than wanting sheer power over others. This brings the responsibility of leading others towards this higher attainment of consciousness.

In negativity you could have the need for power run away with you and can become rather tyrannical, trying to be the 'Big Boss'. Watch out for impulsive actions that can lead to trouble.

You want to be a success but you would prefer to leave nitty-gritty details to others and look at the broad picture only. You help loved ones in their times of trouble.

The Spiritual Purpose for 1

The key to higher awareness is through the expression of individualization of self. You will want to set the pace in things spiritual, and your task is to lead the way, many times where no person has gone before. Do not fear, this is your forte – you are very self-orientated and have the strength to cope. Beware of being overly self-confident, though, as you actually cannot deal with 'every' situation, much as you may think you can.

Some will want to follow your strong lead, to the detriment of their own personal spiritual growth. You must always encourage them to seek within themselves and not take your findings as gospel.

Vowel Number 2

A follower rather than a leader, you are likely to be the peace-maker and restorer of balance, for this is what your past lives have prepared you to do. You love to have companionship, affection, friendship and love. Marriage is definitely for you, and a divorce would be particularly hard for you to cope with. You like being part of a team of people; a co-operative situation is best for you.

In negativity you can overdo the tact and helpfulness and become everybody's doormat. You can be over-sensitive and easily hurt. Discipline is not for you, nor can you discipline others.

But you have much love and affection to give to others and you get what you want and need by being persuasive rather than being heavy-handed. Take the opportunities that come your way, or others may take them from you.

The Spiritual Purpose for 2

The key to higher awareness is through the expression of partnership. This means you have to go with the flow rather than creating your own. Taking whatever is doled out is difficult but it gives you time to take stock of yourself. You have to develop the skill of the diplomat by being careful and tactful in all your contacts with others. It is doubtful that you will start any spiritual concept, but rather take up what others have started and make it work. This is really a purpose that is designed to be of use in future lives. It will all stand you in good stead in the long term. Try not to react to things in an emotional manner, it won't help.

Vowel Number 3

You delight in making others happy and probably like to make them laugh. You will do this with the aid of your witty and friendly self-expression, usually vocal. But you can express it in other artistic ways such as writing or acting. You will never forget your duty, for this is the lesson you have learned in your previous lives and you will know that you are helping yourself by helping others.

In negativity your talking can be rather compulsive and critical of others. In turn you may be very thin-skinned when criticized yourself. Don't be too easy-going or you will never accomplish anything in this life.

In all this helping of others do not forget about yourself and your needs. You want a nice home with beautiful objects around you and that takes time and energy to get and make. You probably lead a very active social life.

The Spiritual Purpose for 3

The key to higher awareness is through the expression of the joy of living. 3 is the number through which you can learn to communicate happiness and joy in the wonderful things of the spirit. You may use any form of communication to do this, from words to pictures. Do not jump hither and thither too much or you may lose the chance of making definite spiritual progress in this life.

Focus your attention on things of a higher nature and absorb what you learn. It is your job in life to give it out to others in a form which they can understand. Yours is the ability to communicate, so use it to help other people in their search for spirituality.

Vowel Number 4

You are likely to love order and routine. A place for everything and everything in its place. Your lifestyle is run like clockwork and is tidy, neat and well-ordered. You really only want to be involved with things that are conventional. You are so methodical that you usually win success. You stand for dependability in this world of chaos, and people look to you to bring order into any system.

In negativity you can be narrow-minded and rigid. You can also become so engrossed in your fanatical methods that you can go over the top and become ridiculous.

Don't take life quite so seriously. Take time to relax a little. Your logicality and practicality are boons to many organizations, but you may be disturbed when inevitable changes come along, destroying your carefully built-up systems. Never mind, it gives you a chance to rebuild.

The Spiritual Purpose for 4

The key to higher awareness is through the expression of all that is solid, practical and what could rather oddly be called 'down-to-earth' spirituality. This is usually done through some form of religion that has rather set ideas, dogmas and tenets to be rigidly observed. These days it is not always churchy-type religions but could be some new sect or a Westernized Eastern religion which has set forms of worship. 4s are usually happier to have a set of rules to follow. 4s also have strong will-power and should be careful that they don't use this to dominate others, for all should be free to find their own way and not be forced to another's way. Please remember, 4s, there are many roads that lead to God.

Vowel Number 5

Freedom isn't just a word to you, you want it in all parts of your life. Even in partnerships you need some space and freedom to be yourself. What really suits you best is to be foot-loose and fancy free, travelling life's highways and experiencing anything there is to be experienced. Adventure is a necessity to you. You don't really like to be governed by tradition.

In negativity you can jump from one thing to another too often. You quickly get rid of the old and put on the new. The new will rarely hold your attention for long. You may have difficulty taking on responsibility.

You are not fond of people who have a narrow view of life, for yours is wide open to everything new and exciting. You are very versatile and resourceful. Your ideas are usually very progressive. Others may not care for them.

The Spiritual Purpose for 5

The key to higher awareness is through the expression of constructive freedom. Every situation presented to you should be used for spiritual growth. You may start many things now that will be completed in other lifetimes. You may hate to be in any situation which appears to tie you down or not allow you to express your own ideas, but this can bring discipline. Remember, freedom without discipline leads to frivolous wasting of time and effort. Make use of your freedom – constructively.

Vowel Number 6

You are likely to be committed to home and family, where you can show your loyalty understanding and affection. This is what you learned in previous lives and now you must pass it on to others. Beauty and harmony are likely to surround you in your life, and peace is paramount. You would like best to be respected for the way you take on and handle responsibility.

In negativity you can love people too well, that is to say you smother-love them and don't allow them self-expression and space. Learn to let go.

When your love is controlled and unconditional you give much friendship, love and affection. You are deeply emotional and likely to express this. When sacrifice is necessary you are capable of making it, and your ability to serve others is never doubted. Don't become resentful.

The Spiritual Purpose for 6

The key to higher awareness is through the expression of the concept of universal brotherhood. Here you must learn to develop the quality of love that expects no return. 'Fair play' means more than mere words to you, and your own actions will always be taken with them in mind. You will often find yourself rushing to defend an under-dog who is being attacked.

These high-minded actions in your life will reflect the highest consciousness, which our world sometimes calls 'Christ Consciousness'. You are likely to let this show within the home environment where it will have the best chance of success. Share your expression through the beautiful home you are capable of creating.

Vowel Number 7

Even if married you can remain unmarried, for it is hard for your loved one to break through your rather cool exterior. You are not very able to express emotions outwardly, although you may think about this – and so many of the other things of life – inwardly. You have learned this separateness in other lives, probably as some kind of hermit, and you still need a lot of space and peace.

In negativity you can be timid, withdrawn and very shy, and have trouble having conversations with people. Your adaptability is not too good and you can be secretive. Watch out you don't stay in the land of dreams.

You want to develop your inner resources and learn deep truths. Don't forget that your resultant philosophy should benefit others as you pass along. The business life may not be for you, nor activity or lively adventures. You can be rather solitary.

The Spiritual Purpose for 7

The key to higher awareness is through the expression of intuition. Many on this vibration seek to enter religious orders, but this is only hiding from your purpose, as is making much of your sensitivity. The latter is the downfall of many, making them shy and introverted.

The work that has to be done is outside the restrictions of religious groups. Probably fear is the greatest thing to conquer, because many times the work of this life is within the psychic and occult fields, which are often despised.

Communication with higher sources is possible and much wonderful inspiration can be received. Do give yourself plenty of opportunity to be alone and meditate on your higher awareness.

Vowel Number 8

You can be called on in this life to handle very large events and run great organizations. You can do this, for in your previous lives you have drummed up enough ambition. Now you must use it to drive you on to sustained effort. You are likely to want power, status, riches and success, and they could very well be yours for the taking, and keeping.

In negativity you could be too domineering and expect too much of other people. Your constant striving for material success can exclude thoughts of anything, or anyone, else. Sad, for you are the loser, you are here to learn that other people have needs and emotions.

If you learn this lesson well it will benefit you, for then you can bring out what is best in them. Be wholehearted to gain the rewards of life.

The Spiritual Purpose for 8

The key to higher awareness is through self-discipline and control. The 8 is the number through which you learn this control. Although it is the number of monetary gain and material success, you have to learn iron control of your circumstances, and this in turn can be applied to your inner life. When defeated, you can learn to accept losing gracefully. In success you can learn to use your success to benefit others and lead them.

Be ready, 8s, for anything life can throw at you. You are here to learn to cope and pass through testing situations which are your initiation into the life spiritual.

Vowel Number 9

You have a tendency to fly away – be careful that you don't become so heavenly that you are no earthly good. This may happen because you have had other lives as adepts and masters and now have a powerfully intuitive and vivid imagination. Although you seem distant to others you are truly, deep down, very warm-hearted and loving. You also need love. Remember, you have to show it to get it.

In negativity you may be critical and moody. There is much conflict between your ambitions and the higher spirituality that is calling you. You may express your emotions too strongly for other mere mortals.

You have talents of a considerable nature and sometimes you share these with others. Remember to get a balance between heaven and earth. Don't let your only existence be in the mind; there's a wonderful world out here and we need you.

The Spiritual Purpose for 9

The key to higher awareness is through the expression of giving without expectation of reward. This can be a physically hard purpose, and care should be taken not to tire yourself out rushing around helping everyone who asks. Learn to say 'no' occasionally. You should have enough wisdom from your past lives to know when this can be done. You should be finishing a task started long ago in an earlier lifetime. Save your strength for this important task. With spending so much of your time seeing to others' needs, some may think you impractical and unworldly. They don't realize the expansion of consciousness this work brings.

Note for Numerologist
If the Vowel Number is 11, please note that sometimes people reject the hardships of a Master Number and revert to the single digit of 2 (1 + 1). Point this out to the sitter and give them the reading for 2 as well as 11. They are more likely to accept the 2, as few can cope with a Master Number's demands.

Vowel Number 11

You have a definite understanding of the ways of this world, and maybe the next as well. Many may wonder at your wisdom and knowledge, how you came by it without (seemingly) really trying. It is because of your many previous lives. You are much more likely to veer towards the spiritual things of this life and want to give unstintingly of yourself to the peoples of this world. You prefer this to giving to individuals, and may become one of the world's great gurus or teachers.

In negativity you may suffer from nervous tension because you are so aware of things at a high level. You can handle your emotions very badly and be altogether too sensitive for your own good. Beware of self-deception.

You are likely to dream utopian dreams, be very intuitive and inspire many people. Your inner strength and devotion to your chosen causes will see you through.

The Spiritual Purpose for 11

The key to higher awareness is through the expression of illumination. That is, teaching the illumination you have been lucky enough to receive in many other lives. Now is the time to pass it on to other people. The trouble is that you may try to do this in the most impractical of ways and be seriously misunderstood. So come down to earth and remember that we more simple mortals have not got your breadth of vision. We cannot appreciate your idealist notions of a wonderful world with everyone only doing good things. To achieve any success you might have to pare your ideas down a little to get them accepted.

Note for Numerologist
If the Vowel Number is 22, please note that sometimes people reject the hardships of a Master Number and revert to the single digit of 4 (2 + 2). Point this out to the sitter and give them the reading for 4 as well as 22. They are more likely to accept the 4, as few can cope with a Master Number's demands.

Vowel Number 22

You are somebody who would really like to make a significant contribution to this planet and possibly be remembered long after you have gone. You have the ability to do just this, for yours is the number of the master builder. It would be more likely this world-shattering contribution will be humanitarian in nature, for you have had many lives and are likely to know you have a special mission to accomplish.

In negativity you can be too dominating. You can suffer from nervous tension. You can have many wonderful notions and ideas and yet never seem to be able to bring them into being.

It is likely you could be a builder, diplomat or engineer in this life – and a good one. Keep your eyes firmly on your goals, deviating neither right nor left. There is little you could not achieve in this life should you set your mind on it. These goals are really the fulfilment of your life (and past lives), and bring benefit to others.

The Spiritual Purpose for 22

The key to higher awareness is through the expression of the master builder. Your dream is to have an ideal world where all are equal and treated equally. It is highly unlikely that this can be brought about, but you will try by expressing your humanitarian ideals and trying to get the rest of us to realize them. You have the capacity to be practical and build fine organizations to improve the world, but you must be prepared to face every difficulty imaginable and overcome it. You have to be resourceful and accept the responsibility of power. Your lesson is to do this without succumbing to corruption of your ideals.

✷

Consonant Number

This number is not as important in a reading as the first three we have already covered. Indeed, some numerologists ignore it altogether. I have discovered that it seems to hide deep wishes, hopes and desires. I've christened it 'The Twist in the Tail', but for our purposes have kept to the easier title of Consonant Number.

This 'twist in the tail' does seem to answer why someone who is set onto one path sometimes breaks out into another, for a shorter or longer time, or perhaps has fits and starts of which reveal the nature of the Consonant Number. An example might be a 1 who suddenly goes all broody and starts the homemaking of a 6. Or a 7 who is constantly communing with heavenly things yet suddenly tries to start a very material business.

At other times it can twist with a vengeance and can screw things right up. I feel this 'twist' is meant to bring tension and variety into a person's existence, which in turn brings the lessons we have to learn. If we were all staid and unchangeable we would never learn and progress. It is an unassailable fact that we learn by conflict. Unalloyed happiness does not do much to move us forward. So we set up conflicts for ourselves to keep us on our toes.

All our numbers do this for us, as we see later, but for now this Consonant Number gives us a first clue.

✱
Consonant Number Charts

Consonant Number 1

This represents the secret wish that what you would like to be is a cool, calm and collected individual, able to handle everything and everyone with ease and poise. You would like to be seen to be an impeccable dresser and be thought of as somebody who really knows what's what and who's who. It takes some very hard work, but this wish could come true.

Inner Spiritual Personality for 1

This number shows that you have an ability to be individual and stand on your own. You do not always need to have a leader and could even become the leader yourself in certain circumstances. Have confidence in your own enlightenment.

Consonant Number 2

This represents a secret wish not to be noticed too much. You may tend to wear very simple clothes, classic styles that blend in with the crowd. You like also to be thought of as a good listener, completely wise, as this brings others to your side. Don't overdo all this or you may just land up being dull and uninteresting. Everyone needs a little colour.

Inner Spiritual Personality for 2

This number shows that you have an ability to work well in group situations, perhaps in an awareness group or meditation group. Your spirituality may make more headway in these types of situations rather than if you try to go it alone.

Consonant Number 3

This represents a secret wish to be the centre of every social gathering. You would like to be thought a great conversationalist and story-teller. Practise and you can be just that. Be careful, though, that your chatter isn't just gossip and exaggeration. You would also like to be thought of as having a magnetic personality which draws everyone to you.

Inner Spiritual Personality for 3

This number shows that you have an ability to communicate your ideas about spirituality if you try. So attempt it in a small way. If you cannot bear the thought of facing crowds, do so on a personal, one-to-one basis. You never know what great work you can accomplish this way.

Consonant Number 4

This represents a secret wish to be of great service to the world. You wish to be thought of as an honest, upright, sober citizen, and you may have a yen to be on your local council where you can serve your local community. Why not?

Inner Spiritual Personality for 4

This number shows that you have an ability to help build up something really worthwhile. It could be a healing sanctuary or an esoteric group. Whatever you try to do could be of enormous help to others and help your own spiritual growth at the same time.

Consonant Number 5

This represents a secret wish to be sexy, witty and exciting. You would like to be thought of as a great dresser and well-travelled person. Nothing is stopping you, just go out and choose the clothes and stop off at the travel agents to pick up a few leaflets. Freedom can be yours, with a little effort.

Inner Spiritual Personality for 5

This number shows that you have an ability to demonstrate constructive freedom. Many think freedom means not having anything to do. You can show that it is much more than that. It is the freedom to choose to do what is necessary to help your fellow man and raise your own consciousness.

Consonant Number 6

This represents a secret wish to take on responsibility, particularly where the family is concerned, where you would like to be thought of as the one who protects and makes everyone comfortable. Well why not? It's quite easy, as others usually want someone else to take responsibility.

Inner Spiritual Personality for 6

This number shows that you have an ability to show unconditional love. This will mainly be possible through home and family circumstances, but can also extend to all the world. Love is the basis of everything, and as such this is a wonderful inner spiritual personality to express.

Consonant Number 7

This represents a secret wish to be mysterious. You would like to be thought of as the philosophical thinker or the solitary mystic. Give yourself a little time and space and you can delve into your inner self. It's no good being mysterious without something to be mysterious about.

Inner Spiritual Personality for 7

This number shows that you have an ability to be mystical, psychic or telepathic, or all three. It means you are sensitive to things of a higher vibration than the one we all see. Don't be frightened by this, some wonderful inspiration which helps us all may be given to you.

Consonant Number 8

This represents a secret wish to be a big business tycoon. Well, successful in business anyway. You would like to be thought of as someone who is strong and powerful, particularly in the world of commerce. This wish takes some very hard work to bring about, but with effort can be fulfilled.

Inner Spiritual Personality for 8

This number shows that you have an ability to understand that wealth and power, material satisfaction, is an illusion. You may just be the one to help humanitarian associations find the money they desperately need, for you would draw it towards you for the right reason.

Consonant Number 9

This represents a secret wish to be the great humanitarian, selfless in your giving. You also have a sneaky wish to be rather dramatic, striking and notice-able. The first can be attained by cultivation of the right attitude, and as for the latter – just go out and treat yourself to some daring clothes or a change in the way you wear your hair.

Inner Spiritual Personality for 9

This number shows that you have an ability to help the world in some humani-tarian way. It may be by individual healing or as part of some large organization. It doesn't really matter as long as you show the art of selfless giving to others.

Please remember the previous note on 11s & 22s (*page 22*).

Consonant Number 11

This represents a secret wish to be a great visionary. You also would like to be thought of as someone who strikes a blow for any kind of equal opportunity. You would like to live life on a higher, more spiritual level than seems possible. Take some time for yourself and you could do and be all you wish.

Inner Spiritual Personality for 11

This number shows that you have an ability to attain illumination. You could understand what this world is all about – and not only this world but that higher dimension to which we all aspire – and pass that knowledge on to others.

Consonant Number 22

This represents a secret wish to right all the wrongs of the world. You would like to be seen as someone very masterly in your handling of people and situations – to be just a little superhuman. Well, there are plenty of wrongs to right – so get on out there and get stuck in. The superhuman part of you could easily reveal itself.

Inner Spiritual Personality for 22

This number shows that you have an ability to demonstrate practical idealism. You could steer people towards a more spiritual way of living and build a better spiritual life for all. Bring your sense of balance to any situation you happen to be in.

Birthday
Numbers

There are many more numbers which have meaning in numerology, and we will be looking at them in later chapters. There is, however, one more number to add to what I consider to be the most important numbers in doing any reading. Do you remember that glass of water to which different colours were added to make a new colour? Well, the numbers we have studied, and now the one we are adding, the actual Birthday Number, are the ones that make up the predominant colour of the glass of water.

Birthday Numbers, as the name suggests, are the actual day (not month or year) on which a person was born. They do not so much work on their reduction but more on the actual numbers that make them up. For example, a date such as the 17th is made up of a 1 and a 7. Remember the meanings of 1 and 7 individually, and then blend them. This is what gives the meaning for double numbers in a birth date.

Birthday Numbers are only a small consideration, a tiny drop of colour in our glass of water. Though other numbers may be seemingly of more importance (such as, in my opinion, the Consonant Number), you must make up your own mind when you have gained experience in doing readings. Numerology is about always discovering new traits and energies.

The Birthday Number charts below give Keywords for the positive and negative energies associated with a birthday number.

★
Birthday Number Charts

1	Positive	Having new ideas, resolute, inventive and creative, self-dependent
	Negative	Jealous, dominating
2	Positive	Loves company, enjoys music, readily affected by surroundings
	Negative	Can be hurt easily, not much confidence
3	Positive	Good companion, many talents, bright-witted
	Negative	Gets bored quickly, prone to over-imagination
4	Positive	Industrious, constant and true, life is well planned
	Negative	Tactless, uncooperative, reserved with others
5	Positive	Bright-witted, many-faceted nature, highly enthusiastic
	Negative	Impulsive, slap-dash, too self-assured
6	Positive	Home-loving, helpful, has loving nature
	Negative	Shy, timid, unable to be content
7	Positive	Likes perfection, will analyse everything, psychic abilities
	Negative	Self comes first, criticizes everything, shows no friendship
8	Positive	Good money abilities, judgement is sound, strength of character
	Negative	Dominant, bosses people around, discouraged easily
9	Positive	Giving, likes to travel, clever, is creative
	Negative	Loses things easily, gets into the wrong set, led by the nose
10	Positive	Able to cope alone, artistic, confident, a law unto themselves
	Negative	Leans on other people, no confidence
11	Positive	Liking for the intellectual, intuition, psychic, altruistic
	Negative	Tight nerves, takes knocks to heart, emotions can go over the top
12	Positive	Friendly, likely to be of help, laid-back, personable
	Negative	Hermit-like, a little 'odd', easily discouraged
13	Positive	Industrious, will to get on, many talents, works with enthusiasm
	Negative	Cool to others, no emotion, not understood
14	Positive	Many-faceted nature, good imagination, works hard, flexible
	Negative	Inconsiderate, erratic, hasty
15	Positive	Well-disposed to help others, big-hearted, accommodating, appreciative of others
	Negative	Reluctant to help others, selfish, agitator

16	Positive	Interested in spiritual ideas, philosophical, intellectual, a mystic
	Negative	Dissatisfied with everything, crosspatch, fusspot
17	Positive	Money comes to you, home-loving, attentive, traditional
	Negative	Blows hot and cold, given to moods, temperamental
18	Positive	Accomplished, capable of leadership, great organizing ability, animated
	Negative	Quarrelsome, very critical, difficult to please
19	Positive	Bounces back, survivor, innovative, all-rounder
	Negative	Downhearted, hair-splitting, stick in the mud
20	Positive	Likes being with people, careful, musically-minded, artistic
	Negative	Inward-looking, too sensitive, apprehensive
21	Positive	Eloquent, disarming, elegant, very charming
	Negative	Grasping, covetous, stingy
22	Positive	Helpful, gives protection, sees the truth, well-balanced
	Negative	Greedy, feather-brained, inflated sense of self-worth
23	Positive	Ethical, conscientious, many-faceted nature
	Negative	Hum-drum, nit-picking, introvert
24	Positive	Careful, busy, dutiful, plenty of energy
	Negative	Green-eyed, uncooperative, fractious
25	Positive	Loves open air, deeply thoughtful, likes perfection
	Negative	Changeable, nervy, sulky
26	Positive	Sacrificial, good parent, likes home life
	Negative	Throws in the towel, no enthusiasm, no tenacity
27	Positive	Loving, great company, wants to get on, bright ideas
	Negative	Trouble-maker, unpleasant with others, quarrelsome
28	Positive	Good will-power, copes alone, lively, unconventional
	Negative	No motivation, dreamer, no grip on reality
29	Positive	Creative, likely to succeed, makes themselves felt
	Negative	Subject to moods, hard to get on with, changeable
30	Positive	Loyal, possessing many gifts, expressive, even-tempered
	Negative	Difficult, all over the place, wants things now, ill-tempered
31	Positive	Tenacious, tireless, constructor, builder
	Negative	No ambition, insecure, easily despondent

Synthesizing What We Have Discovered

Having covered the most important numbers – the Birth Number, the three Name Numbers and the Birthday Number – we now have to get down to making sense of what we have discovered. Quite often I use just these few reductions of numbers as a tool when I start to do a clairvoyant reading. It gives me a quick 'in' to the person. If you want to help somebody discover their path and are short of time, these numbers will give you most of what you need to know.

But reading them is much more than reducing the numbers and reading off the paragraphs from this or any other book. We have spoken before about weighing up one number with another – likening it to the multi-coloured glass of water – and about positive and negative considerations. It would be best to study this more deeply before introducing any further numbers – which will undoubtedly still be Transformers, but of a lesser nature.

✴ Soft and Hard Numbers

All numbers have friction between them because of their different natures, but some conflict more than others. Hopefully you are becoming more accustomed to the general meaning of the numbers by now, so consider 2 and 7, 9 and 8, and 5 and 4. These are numbers of definite conflicting energies. Now consider 2 and 6, 8 and 4, and 1 and 5. What I am going to put forward here is not invariable, but notice that odd numbers clash with even numbers, whilst odd with odd and even with even do not, or not as much.

I call odd numbers 'soft' and even numbers 'hard'. This does not relate to the character of the person, but is just a way of remembering this idea. It is a

58

quick way of looking through somebody's numbers and seeing if trouble is lurking there.

✷

Conflict and Harmony

We have spoken about people choosing their own names before they ever arrive here on earth. They are chosen with great care, along with the astrological moment of their birth. It is a very complex matter and we earthly astrologers and numerologists have not got all the answers, only a method of gaining some information for ourselves and our clients. If a person has progressed to a point of great spiritual stature, they will not need such tools to know who they are. But mostly we are not at that point yet – and yet we are at the point where we are curious and needing to know.

The numerologist has to decant the colours in the glass of water back to their original hues, and then, in putting them back together again, see the how and why of each colour as it produces changes and the final outcome.

We have studied positive and negative qualities, and know that a trait may be in the negative or in the process of being changed to the positive. Not only this, but sometimes one finds definite characteristics which pertain to the negative. For instance, 7s, if they choose to turn away from the psychic and mystical, often hide behind the frivolous pursuit of clothes, dancing and good times. They may do this all their lives and will say to you, 'I'm not in the least interested in psychic things.' A 2 may be ultra-shy and have difficulty in finding a partner, which is the very thing they crave.

Positive and negative is fairly easy to deal with, but Conflict and Harmony is a little bit more tricky. As we progress down the numbers, so they affect the total picture less. The most important is the Birth Number, with the Whole Name Number and the Vowel Number having a very strong effect, whilst the Consonant Number and Birthday Number have even less.

✶
Conflict and Harmony Charts

Please Note

What is important to remember here is that you are comparing each number in the chart with another one – that is, Birth Number with the Whole Name Number, a Vowel Number with the Consonant Number, or any other two numbers in a chart. It is used to see if the two numbers sit comfortably together or cause disharmony.

You will see I have included 11 and 22. Also note that I have not repeated, say, 9 with 7, as 7 with 9 comes first in the list. Just look for the two numbers together, as the meaning is the same whichever comes first.

Please Also Note

This list of Conflict and Harmony readings is not for deciding if you are compatible with anybody else in a relationship. We cover that later in full (*pages 134–46*). This is to find the Conflict and Harmony within your (or someone else's) own chart. Please study this carefully and apply it to any readings you do.

1 with 1

Harmonious: but more than one 1 in a chart will enforce the 1 potential, possibly driving it into the negative – of being overbearing, even dictatorial, especially in youth.

1 with 2

Conflicting: 1 stands alone and 2 always needs partnership. It leads to difficulties as to which to choose.

1 with 3

Harmonious: 3 gives the ability to express the 1. 1 can sometimes have good ideas and not be able to get them over to others. The 3 rectifies this.

1 with 4

Harmonious: the 4 settles the 1 down to hard work rather than expecting every-body else to do it. The 1 stops the 4 getting too bogged down in details.

1 with 5

Harmonious and *Conflicting*: both like to get out and about, see what is over the hill, but 1 is much more serious about getting to a specific destination, whereas 5 just likes to wander.

1 with 6

Conflicting: 1 stands alone, whereas 6 wants to be in a family circle. The 1 tends to think of itself, but the 6 constantly thinks of others.

1 with 7

Conflicting: both like to work alone, but 7 is usually considering spiritual matters whilst 1 is interested in more earthly matters.

1 with 8

Harmonious: both pursue material gain, and 1 offers the 8 leadership qualities. But beware, if it falls into the negative of both the person becomes self-centred and selfish.

1 with 9

Conflicting: 9 might give away all that 1 manages to gain. But if 1 uses the 9 posi-tively it could bring good creative results.

1 with 11

Conflicting: 1 seeks outer potential whilst the 11 is seeking the inner self.

1 with 22

Conflicting: 1 can be rather self-seeking whilst 22 seeks success for the greater good of all.

2 with 2

Conflicting: 2 tends not to be able to make decisions without others' help; it can mean a weakening if there is more than one 2.

2 with 3

Harmonious: 3 helps the 2 to communicate whilst the 3 helps the 2 to come forward more.

2 with 4

Harmonious: the diplomacy of 2 helps the 4 to understand people, and 4 brings order to the 2.

2 with 5

Conflicting: 2 wants to stay put whilst 5 wants to roam. This can cause confusion within and make life very difficult.

2 with 6

Harmonious: both want to be in the bosom of the family and have a beautiful home.

2 with 7

Conflicting: 2 wants to share with another, 7 more often wants to be alone. 2 looks for more material comforts and finds 7s concern with earthly things disconcerting.

2 with 8

Conflicting: 8 is concerned with big business; 2 is more concerned with smaller home issues. 2 is too sensitive for business.

2 with 9

Harmonious: both like giving to others, although 9 might find 2's giving on rather a small scale.

2 with 11

Harmonious: 2 loves to have a harmonious, peaceful space, in which 11 can dream of higher things. But 11 can get fed up with 2's down-to-earthness. (Remember, 2 is the 'backing off' number of 11.)

2 with 22

Conflicting: 2 can hold back the leadership of 22. 2 does not like to be in a large group, whereas 22 thrives on it.

3 with 3

Conflicting: the frivolous side of 3 can be quite overwhelming. Can even stop the communication that is the life-blood of 3.

3 with 4

Conflicting: the bright, witty charm of 3 conflicts with the seemingly dull, plodding 4.

3 with 5

Harmonious: both are outgoing and social. Beware this does not descend into frittering life away with no good results.

3 with 6

Harmonious: 6 brings love, balance and responsibility to the 3's social life, and 3 takes 6 out and about a bit.

3 with 7

Conflicting: 3 is gregarious and 7 a loner. But 7 can make use of the communicating 3 to explain their deep, deep thoughts.

3 with 8

Conflicting: the socialite 3 might hold the 8 back from making serious progress. Yet all is not lost if the 8 uses the communication of the 3.

3 with 9

Harmonious: 3 helps 9 express its givingness and become more social. 3, which can be very self-seeking, is helped by the kindness of 9.

3 with 11

Harmonious: dreaming 11 needs to express its deep illuminations, which is helped by 3's communicating ability. 3 needs the spirituality of 11.

3 with 22

Conflicting: 3 wants to play while 22 is a serious number with a serious task to do. 22 must make use of 3's ability to communicate.

4 with 4

Conflicting: 4's limitations are doubly bad and it can make for misery and frustration. Extra effort is needed here to work hard and succeed. A very hard lesson here.

4 with 5

Conflicting: freedom-loving 5 just does not go with organized, a-place-for-every-thing 4. A great deal of conflict to work out here.

4 with 6

Harmonious: 4 helps 6 build, particularly home nests, but 4 can find the love expressed by 6 a bit difficult to understand.

4 with 7

Harmonious: 4 can bring steadiness to 7. 7s analytical approach is somewhat similar to 4's ability to organize.

4 with 8

Conflicting: 4 and 8 are very similar and it means getting rather self-centred and stuck in rigidity, plus only being interested in business.

4 with 9

Conflicting: the generosity of 9 conflicts with the somewhat tight-fistedness of 4, which may only be trying to conserve resources.

4 with 11

Conflicting: 4 holds 11 too heavily down on the ground and does not let 11's imagination fly free. 11 too dreamy for organized 4.

4 with 22

Harmonious: remember, however, that 4 is the 'backing off' number of 22. 4's presence might tempt the person to dive for the cover of the lower vibration more readily. With strength of (22) character, however, it can work out well.

5 with 5

Conflicting: the propensity of 5 for the excess in food, drink, drugs and sex is heightened to a point that is positively dangerous. Strong control is needed here.

5 with 6

Conflicting: 6 stays home whilst 5 always wants to see what is over the next hill. Difficult to reconcile.

5 with 7

Conflicting: 5's almost zany worldly interest conflicts with the inner, quieter and more analytical approach of 7.

5 with 8

Conflicting: 8 is steady in its aims to get on in life, whilst 5 is usually scattered and not able to concentrate on any one thing for long.

5 with 9

Conflicting: 9 always wants to be giving to others; 5 can be selfish in its desire for freedom. 5 can help 9 to express its ideas.

5 with 11

Conflicting: 5 can't sit still long enough to listen to the deeper illuminations of 11.

5 with 22

Conflicting: 5 can't stay around long enough to see the big building plans of 22 through.

6 with 6

Conflicting: the 6 strengthened turns inward too much and takes on too many responsibilities, forgetting self altogether.

6 with 7

Conflicting: 7 is busy looking inward to higher matters, 6 is wanting to care about homely, worldly things.

6 with 8

Conflicting: 8 wants to be in business and 6 wants to be at home – can work if the business is run from home or to do with homemaking.

6 with 9

Harmonious: both want to give to others – but it can be that the self is never seen as needing something, or is never given time.

6 with 11

Harmonious: 11 can share with 6 the moral sense of love and responsibility. 6 brings beauty to the 11.

6 with 22

Harmonious: both are concerned with caring for others, 6 in a small way and 22 on a grand scale.

7 with 7

Conflicting: can trigger the 'differentness' into complete eccentricity. Feet are always off the ground and head stuck in heavenly matters.

7 with 8

Conflicting: 8 has its head stuck into business and worldly matters, whilst 7 is off investigating mystical things.

7 with 9

Conflicting: 7 is within, 9 is more outward going. 7 can bring a spiritual outlook to 9's givingness.

7 with 11

Harmonious: both are equally dreamy and interested in the spiritual aspect of life, but this combination can leave them stranded in mid-air.

7 with 22

Conflicting: mystical 7 cannot deal too well with 22's material pursuits. With the nervous tension of 22 it can lead to vacillation.

8 with 8

Conflicting: enforces the materialistic pursuits of 8. Less likelihood of learning the lesson of 8, which is to learn the illusion of materiality.

8 with 9

Conflicting: unless 8 uses its business acumen to find money for charity, life becomes confusing: to make money or to give it away?

8 with 11

Conflicting: the spiritual possibilities 11 sees hold 8 back from gaining success in material business pursuits.

8 with 22

Harmonious: enhance each other's chances of success in material and business pursuits, though 22 is broader and possibly more spiritual in outlook than 8.

9 with 9

Conflicting: everything might be given away, leaving nothing for the self. Constant tiredness could be here as well.

9 with 11

Harmonious: 11 will bring the spiritual to bear in the ways that 9 gives to others. A pleasant combination.

9 with 22

Harmonious: 22 works to gain material and spiritual gifts for 9 to give away. At least 9 has something to give!

11 with 11

Conflicting: the head is completely lost in the clouds and the feet never touch earth. Practicality is at a minimum and little actually accomplished, although there may be a wealth of good ideas.

11 with 22

Conflicting: 11's aim is spiritual achievement, whilst 22's is more material. A great deal of nervous tension would be experienced and cause much difficulty. 11 must try to be more practical to help the 22.

These meanings are not set in concrete. As you will see sometimes the conflict can be turned into harmony if used in a positive way. This again means that people will say 'I am not like that' when really they need to be congratulated for overcoming the conflict that may have once raged within them.

In others it will still be raging; it is the numerologist's job to point out this possibility and seek to help the person sort it out.

Another interesting fact you may have noted is that two of the same numbers is not harmonious. This may seem strange, but two of the same number strengthens and enhances the vibrations both positively and negatively. Unfortunately it is usually negatively. Always point this out and try to encourage the person to use these energies to strengthen the positive aspects of the given number.

In the next section we will try out some syntheses to find out what kind of characters our mythical John and Jane possess, and then you can move on to your own chart.

✷

Practice in Synthesizing

You will recall that our mythical John's numbers were:

- Birth Number 4
- Whole Name Number 5
- Vowel Number 22
- Consonant Number 1
- Birthday Number 23

John's Conflicts and Harmonies

Let us see what harmonies and conflicts we can find here.

4 with 5

Conflicting: freedom-loving 5 just does not go with organized, a-place-for-everything 4. A great deal of conflict to work out here.

4 with 22

Harmonious: remember, however, that 4 is the 'backing off' number of 22. 4's presence might tempt the person to dive for the cover of the lower vibration more readily. With strength of (22) character, however, it can work out well.

5 with 22

Conflicting: 5 can't stay around long enough to see the big building plans of 22 through.

Two not too good and one OK. We could have guessed that 22 – 4 would be OK, as 22 is the Backing Off Number of 4. But note the warning – it might drive him into the 4 rather than towards expressing the Master Number. Yet it is his soul energy, and that might mean he stays with the 22.

But 4 and 5 and 5 with 22: The antitheses of each other. And John's Birthday Number repeats the 5 (2 + 3 when reduced) and meaning:

Positive	Ethical, conscientious, many-faceted nature
Negative	Humdrum, nit-picking, introverted

His 'twist in the tail', his Consonant Number, is 1, which will make him suddenly want to lead or pioneer, not a 4 thing – but it is a 22 desire.

John may have had a difficult life because he has never known whether to stay put in a rather dull routine or pack his bags and travel the world. To live a solid married life or dissipate his emotions all over the place. On top of this, as I mentioned before, I have spotted that John has other difficulties with which to contend. I will not go into details here, but his Birth Number of 13/4 means that he has a Karmic Debt to repay and work out in this life (*see section on Karmic Debts, pages 94–6*). Indeed, this may be the whole reason why John has such a difficult set of numbers.

Is it right to tell someone if you find such conflict or debt in their numbers? It certainly can be, for this was exactly how I myself came to be able to accept my rather upside-down life and begin to set it right, for I have just such a debt on my own number.

Of course, how you word your reading is of great importance. Point out the good and the bad, and then suggest what this might mean and how a person might come to terms with their energies. If they have come to you looking for a Soul Reading in the first place they are probably well on the way to needing to know this information for their ultimate spiritual progression. Use your knowledge of the numbers to temper the way you tell the person about them. 2s are timid, 5s don't often really want to know, 3s will tell you, 7s will go introvert on you, etc.

Jane's Conflicts and Harmonies

Let's do another exercise with Jane's numbers.

- Birth Number 6
- Whole Name Number 1
- Vowel Number 6
- Consonant Number 4
- Birthday Number 1

1 with 6

Conflicting: 1 stands alone, whereas 6 wants to be in a family circle. The 1 tends to think of itself, but the 6 constantly thinks of others.

6 with 6

Conflicting: the 6 strengthened turns inward too much and takes on too many responsibilities, forgetting self altogether.

And Birthday 1:

Positive	New ideas, resolute, inventive and creative, self-dependent
Negative	Jealous, dominating

Again, we have rather a lot of conflict. Well in truth, all charts have conflict, though some have less than others. Jane's 6s will make her want to home-make like mad; she'll want balance and love to abound, but her 1 Whole Name Number, backed up by her Birthday Number 1, will also make her want to be individual, to stand out in a crowd. If the crowd is her family she may cause upsets rather than balance. The 'twist in the tail' Consonant Number of 4 is not very significant in Jane's case, because she will be a hard worker already.

Jane at least has no Karmic Debts that I can see; it may well be that she can turn it all into the positive of the energies involved. The 1 may balance out with the 6. I would advise her to run a business from home, perhaps on a computer network where she can interact with others from the safety of her home. She has the pioneer 1 in her to take to modern technology. Indeed, I always advise 6s to work from home or in some kind of family group if at all possible. This 'family group' may not be a conventional nuclear family. I did a reading for an actress with 6s who toured with a group at times and then had to go home to live alone. She hated the latter because she had lost 'her family', the other actors. When I pointed this out it helped her accept it and made life easier for her to deal with.

As we go along learning about further numbers and using some numerological methods to gain more information, we will get more practice in synthesizing the numbers. For now, why don't you cast about among family and friends and synthesize their numbers? You don't have to tell them the results – but I bet they ask! The good thing about this is that, as you already know something of the characteristics of these close folk, you can see if your synthesis is correct. You will be surprised at what is uncovered. Indeed, you can use even just the Birth Number to get a handle on a person. Of course, like all these kinds of tools, there is a percentage that just don't hang together. Particularly if you only use the basic numbers. But I would say in my experience something like 90 per cent and above ring true. Often, if you know the person, they may not see it as true, even if you can see that it is. It is not always possible for us to accept the truth about ourselves. Offer the reading's finding and then let it sink in. I have found that a sitter will come back later, agreeing after having thought it through.

Maturity
Number

Most of our numbers come with us as we arrive on this earth or soon after. However, there is one number which, although derived from these other numbers, does not make its entrance until later in life. This is the Maturity Number.

In Soul Numerology we do not use age – such as 18 or 21 – to gauge maturity. Instead we take the age at which the person genuinely matures, and this may be at any time in their life. Some are old souls who are mature in childhood; others have not really matured when it is time for them to leave this earth.

Here we are talking about *spiritual maturity* – and that usually comes after the world has done its best to knock us into shape. Those who use these experiences wisely begin to look into deeper matters, asking questions and seeking knowledge of the spirit. Others skim across the surface and tend to find no meaning anywhere, often going on to make the same mistakes again and again.

All the energies of our numbers bring us lessons which are mostly of a harsh nature, although some may seem to be not so difficult. Think of an 8 finding it easy to bring good fortune and wealth to themselves. Most of us would not call this a hard lesson, but remember the poor little rich girls. Wealth is not always an easy lesson.

So how can we say when a person has reached maturity? I usually leave it to the person to decide for themselves. Somewhere deep inside, they know.

Here are some pointers. Women usually mature before men. I think it is the fact that they bear the children and feel the responsibility more clearly. I know it taught (a decidedly impatient) me patience, and very quickly. Today some fathers are having to take over this responsibility, and I find it makes an enormous difference to them. Perhaps they will mature earlier, like women.

I usually put the age for women to mature as in their thirties or forties. I have been forced to note how many times it is this age group that seeks advice from people such as myself.

In men, if they have been through the hoops of life it can be at the same sort of age, but mostly it is later, even in their fifties and sixties. I mean no insult by this, gentlemen, it is just my experience. Perhaps you have to be out there in the world too much and haven't had time to let the leavening of life's difficulties go deep within. Conversely, women, who now are in the workplace more, may find they do not attain this spiritual maturity until later in life.

So I'm not talking about sexual maturity or mental/intellectual maturity, but a realization that there is more to life than was first thought. Something more subtle, more meaningful. This is the moment when the energies of the Maturity Number kick in, but don't forget there are always the few who can mature much earlier, even in their teens. As mentioned, these are usually 'old souls' who bring back much experience from other lives – this should be reflected in their numbers.

This is a drop of a new colour to that glass of water, which if totally different to the other numbers, may have quite an effect.

Finding the Maturity Number

We now use the numbers at the ♥ sign in the Birth Number chart and the ♦ in the Whole Name Number Workout Charts. That is to say, the first complete number before it is reduced further to make the Birth or Whole Name Numbers. Remember, this could be a single- or double-digit number.

You will recall the Birth Number chart and the Name Number chart. We now use the numbers before the ♥ and the ♦ signs and add these numbers together and reduce.

John's Birth Number at the ♥ was 13 and his Whole Name Number at the ♦ was 32, so:

$$13 + 32 = 45$$
$$4 + 5 = 9$$
$$9 = \text{Maturity Number}$$

So 9 is John's Maturity Number. Check his synthesis and you will see that this addition of a 9 may make him more caring and giving. Now work out Jane's Maturity Number. She has a 15/6 Birth Number and a 10/1 Whole Name Number.

Now work out your own.

★
Maturity Number Charts

Maturity Number 1

You are likely to have to face up to being independent, standing on your own feet. 1 is the number that brings individuality, so learning to cope alone is obviously a sub-lesson that you have to learn in this life. This will help bring strength of character to your mature personality.

Maturity Number 2

You are likely to have to learn about sensitivity – being sensitive to the needs of others and your own sensitivity. This can be a hard lesson, as it may come through insensitive treatment of yourself by others. Sensitivity is beautiful and will enhance your mature personality.

Maturity Number 3

You are likely to have to learn to enjoy life a little more than you have, to find joy in living. This may be done by finding ways of expressing yourself, maybe artistically and/or by bringing enjoyment to others through this expression. It will round out your mature life.

Maturity Number 4

You are likely to have to become aware that there can be limitations placed on one and you have to learn to cope despite them. Try not to carp about these limitations, but rather build a good life having assimilated their lessons. It will mean a stronger you in your mature life.

Maturity Number 5

You are likely suddenly to find you have gained freedom from some factor in your life and you now have to learn to use this freedom constructively and not fritter it away. Freedom is a wonderful thing but it can be wasted, so use it well to enhance your mature life.

Maturity Number 6

You are likely to have to learn to cope with responsibilities, probably of a family nature. This will bring love and affection to the fore, and making use of caring as a means of expressing this love. This lesson will round out your abilities to show love in maturity.

Maturity Number 7

You are likely to want time to yourself to think about things beyond this world. Something will bring about your wish to study and possibly meditate on things of a philosophical nature. This will deepen and bring more spiritual content to your mature life.

Maturity Number 8

You are likely to want to find more material satisfaction and come to understand the gifts of this world. Opportunities may present themselves to gain these gifts, but remember the lesson is to realize they are of this world and therefore transient. Mature recognition of this is important.

Maturity Number 9

You are likely to have to learn the lesson that selfless giving gives great satisfaction in itself. Humanitarian pursuits will attract you, and if you give willingly of yourself you may find a wonderful joy in your mature life. This is a lesson for the higher nature and can be very difficult.

Maturity Number 11

You are likely to have to realize that there is an awareness in you of the higher, more spiritual worlds. This is a Master Number lesson and very difficult if you have not experienced a master vibration before. Try to let this illumination gently permeate your mature self with its revelations.

Maturity Number 22

You are likely to have to learn about high ideals and control of power. This is a Master Number lesson and very difficult if you have not experienced a master vibration before. Try to absorb it slowly and you may build something of great worth during your mature life to benefit others.

Changed Name Number

Here I must refer you back to what I wrote in the chapter about changing names in general. If you change your name for any reason, you will be placing a veil of another energy over your numbers. It will bring some changes but it will not remove the former energies which you have come to experience. Indeed, it could lead you away from your life path and cause you to fail in what you set out to achieve in this life. So take a great deal of thought before changing your name, and perhaps seek out numerologically what it will mean. If there is no choice, as in marriage, then at least be aware of the energy it will bring with it and be prepared. The energy of a Changed Name Number is quite strong and can bring some changes, but remember the basic energies are still there. It is a good thing to know about this change and take it into consideration. An instance could be that it brings the wish for the freedom of the 5 when you are a 6. Or again, the hard work of 4 when you are a possibly physically lazy 7. So look for these new conflicts or harmonies when doing a chart.

★
Finding the Changed Name Number

If the name is completely changed then you must use the same Workout Chart already given for the names on page 25, and re-work the whole name using a chart like the one below. If it is just a married name, then we must go back to our original chart and use the Given Name totals plus a working out of the new surname. This number is nothing to do with whether it will make you compatible with a partner if you marry them, it is another energy added to your own chart and affecting you only.

Name Chart   **Vowel Number** ⇓

.....⑥.......... + ...⑪.......... + ...7.......... =«24» / 6

..... 6 .... / ....11.......... / ....16.............↑....

...1..+..5 .... / ....6..+..5 .... / ....9....+.....7 ....↑....

Name J A N E / R O S E / K I R K B Y ↑

1 ....+...5......... / ....9..+..1.......... / .....2..+..9 + 2 +2 .... ↓

.... 6 .... / ....10............. / ....15............. ↓

...... 6 .... / ....1.......... / ....6 .... ↓

.....⑥.......... + ...①.......... + ...6 .... ↓ =«13» / 4 ↓

                                      Consonant Number ⇑..↓

Add **Vowel** & **Consonant Numbers** between «.» together and reduce «..37» /◆ 10/1

                                  Whole Name Number ⇑

.....⑫/③.......... / ......⑫/③......... **Given Names Totals**

Add the **Vowel** & **Consonant Numbers** of each name separately and write them in the space above

Figure 5

Figure 5 shows our old friend Jane's Name Workout Chart. We can see she has in her Given Names the totals 3 and 3 (that is, her first name Vowel Number, 6, plus first name Consonant Number, 6, makes 12 (1 + 2), which equals 3; her middle name Vowel Number is 11, plus middle name Consonant Number 1, equals 12 (1 + 2), which equals 3). We now add this to her married name below. We DO NOT separate the vowels and consonants, as there is only one new energy here, not three as in the original name.

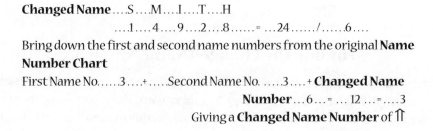

Changed Name ....S....M....I....T....H

            ....1....4....9....2....8......= ...24....../......6....

Bring down the first and second name numbers from the original **Name Number Chart**

First Name No.....3....+.....Second Name No. ....3....+ **Changed Name**

                             Number ...6...= ... 12 ...=....3

                   Giving a **Changed Name Number** of ⇑

Figure 6

If you have a changed name work out your number now.

Changed Name . . . .
. . . . = ... / . . . .

Bring down the first and second name numbers from the original **Name Number Chart**

First Name No. . . . . + ... Second Name No. . . . . + **Changed Name Number** . . . . = ... = ...

Giving a **Changed Name Number** of ⇑

Here are the charts for the energy of a Changed Name, so you can add this factor to Jane's (or anyone else's) synthesis.

✷

Changed Name Charts

Changed Name Number 1

Your new name modifies your vibrations by developing individuality and an ability to cope on your own, alone. If this is also your Birth Number, then you are trying to strengthen this characteristic. But beware it does not drive you into the negative, namely selfishness.

   Keyword: *Individualization* – this does not mean selfishness but learning to be yourself and not relying on others. Inner strength to survive can be found within this vibration. But, as mentioned, beware it does not drive you into the negative.

Changed Name Number 2

Your new name modifies your vibrations by developing duality, the need to learn the art of partnership. If this is also your Birth Number then you are trying to strengthen this characteristic. But beware it does not drive you into the negative, namely shyness.

   Keyword: *Co-operation* – learning to work with others and sometimes sublimating self for the benefit of the whole. It could work in groups as well as on a one-to-one basis. The art of joining in well with others is a good one to choose to learn.

Changed Name Number 3

Your new name modifies your vibrations by developing communication, the ability to express yourself in creative ways. If this is also your Birth Number then you are trying to strengthen this characteristic. But beware it does not drive you into the negative, namely being introverted.

Keyword: *Joy of living* – which you have to make others see through your art, writing, speech or acting, some way that will express the wonder and joy of being alive. In a simple form it may just be talking to a friend or neighbour.

Changed Name Number 4

Your new name modifies your vibrations by developing order, service and the ability to cope with restricting limitations. If this is also your Birth Number then you are trying to strengthen this characteristic. But beware it does not drive you into the negative, namely being a stick in the mud.

Keyword: *Limitation* – that is, developing one's gifts even though difficulties and limitations surround your life. This is the number of the builder who, with patience, erects something worthwhile.

Changed Name Number 5

Your new name modifies your vibrations by developing the gift of understanding freedom. If this is also your Birth Number then you are trying to strengthen this characteristic. But beware it does not drive you into the negative, namely carelessness.

Keyword: *Constructive freedom* – in the wide sense this means developing the ability to handle travel, adventure and unexpected happenings. In another sense it means becoming a bit more outward-going or finding the freedom of the soul.

Changed Name Number 6

Your new name modifies your vibrations by developing responsibility. This is usually expressed through the home and family. If this is also your Birth Number then you are trying to strengthen this characteristic. But beware it does not drive you into the negative, namely being uncaring.

Keyword: *Balance* – through love which can be shown in so many ways, caring for those in your immediate surroundings. This is the best place to learn the lessons of responsibility as you help to bring about harmony and beauty.

Changed Name Number 7

Your new name modifies your vibrations by developing understanding, giving yourself time for introspective thought. If this is also your Birth Number then you are trying to strengthen this characteristic. But beware it does not drive you into the negative, namely being difficult.

Keyword: *Analysis* – thought must be given to those things which do not pertain to this world. In this way you can become a more rounded person with some kind of philosophy which will sustain you through life's tribulations.

Changed Name Number 8

Your new name modifies your vibrations by developing material satisfaction, the ability to draw your needs towards you. If this is also your Birth Number then you are trying to strengthen this characteristic. But beware it does not drive you into the negative, namely being bossy.

Keyword: *Concentration* – in order to gain your end result. The hidden meaning of the 8 is learning that material gain is an illusion, so use any gain with intelligence and love. Don't get lost in the goods materiality provides.

Changed Name Number 9

Your new name modifies your vibrations by developing humanitarianism, the act of giving without expectation of reward. If this is also your Birth Number then you are trying to strengthen this characteristic. But beware it does not drive you into the negative, namely being unhelpful.

Keyword: *Selflessness* – any satisfaction will come from the act of giving to others. This giving may mean helping others or giving of your inner self through some creative art form.

Changed Name Number 11

Your new name modifies your vibrations by developing illumination, a gift from a higher plane than most. If this is also your Birth Number then you are trying to strengthen this characteristic. But beware it does not drive you into the negative, namely being too dreamy.

Keyword: *Illumination* – and nervous tension may be introduced on this vibration. Intuition should be developed and there must be a readiness to mediate between heaven and earth. Inspire others by your own illumination.

Changed Name Number 22

Your new name modifies your vibrations by developing the qualities of a master builder. If this is also your Birth Number then you are trying to strengthen this characteristic. But beware it does not drive you into the negative, namely being too domineering.

Keyword: *Master Builder* – bringing in the possibilities of making high ideals into concrete forms. There is terrific potential in this Master Number but it's hard to live up to. Perhaps there is something you have to build. Nervous tension may be introduced with this number.

Early Development and Early Lesson Numbers

There are two numbers which are particularly important in early life, and may help to explain the way a person felt and acted as a child. They are the Early Development Number, and the Early Lesson Number.

We get the Early Development Number from the simple expedient of adding up the numbers of the first name, to find this special energy given to illuminate the other numbers and find the way to grow during life.

Here is John's Development Number worked out:

$$J \; O \; H \; N$$
$$1 \; 6 \; 8 \; 5 \; = \; 20 \; = \; 2$$

This number can help or hinder early growth by its Conflict or Harmony with the main numbers of the chart. There is one difference to note here, though: If the Development Number is the same as some of the other numbers in a person's chart, it will help the person to bring forward the Positive influences of that number. If it differs from all the other numbers in a person's chart, then you must look to see what sort of conflict or harmony the person can expect.

Early Development Number Charts

Early Development Number 1

This Early Development Number may have caused a fear of rejection in childhood, or you could have been intimidated by others. This has been chosen to bring out your ability to cope alone and not worry about what opinion others may have of you. Be careful this does not develop into dominance of others rather than independence. Take into account the needs of other people. Also in youth you may have depended too much on others. Make sure this does not continue and that you are able to care for yourself. Take the responsibilities of leadership when offered, although your style of leadership may not always be what's expected and could be thought unacceptable.

Early Development Number 2

This Early Development Number means you have to walk the fine line between promoting the welfare of others and not forgetting your own. When young you were likely to have been shy or even retiring in nature, allowing others to come first. This would have been misunderstood and thought to be fear of others. In later life you should have grown more able to cope and not allowed self-effacement to be so strong. You have the ability to be aware of the more subtle messages others give, and should use this gift. Be co-operative and helpful to all, but remember your own needs. Do not fear rejection – go ahead and express friendship.

Early Development Number 3

With this Early Development Number you must learn that however 'way out' and daring your way of expressing yourself is, it is up to others to come to terms with it. Don't worry, that's your way of growing within the self. This, of course, does not mean being rude or over-bearing, but accept the fact that you may come over as being unique, one of a kind.

Your input will vitalize people and make for a more exciting life for them and you. You may have developed this ability of expression as a way of combating childhood shyness. Never fear rejection – go ahead and express your creative feelings.

Early Development Number 4

With this Early Development Number you will have to learn to work within limitations. Hopefully you have learned to do this in a positive manner. If you have only shown frustration then you have not used this number properly. Accept the limitations and don't become downhearted. Sometimes the limitations can be changed, other times you have to live with them. Knowing which is which is what brings about your growth. Try to work in a systematic manner, be practical and work hard. Concentrate on the service you give others rather than the work itself.

Early Development Number 5

With this Early Development Number you have to show adaptability and an ability to look at lots of ideas, gaining knowledge from the many exciting things in this world, yet not falling prey to the physical pleasures that abound. You have to find your feet in a world that offers drink, drugs, sex, etc. so freely and enticingly, and learn how to integrate them into a balanced way of living. Learn to use your energy wisely and don't start things you have no intention of finishing.

Early Development Number 6

With this Early Development Number you will have to learn to shoulder responsibilities and give help whenever it is needed. You must do this without bemoaning the burdens placed upon you, and carry them out with understanding. Contribute to making your home comfortable and stable; offer friendship, love and harmony and learn to accept these things in return with good face. All this must be done by learning to balance one thing against another, learning to judge well about what is needed. In this way you will come to enjoy the happy, balanced and loving environment that will surround you.

Early Development Number 7

With this Early Development Number you will learn to live the life within the self. You must trust the direction that intuition leads you; it is for your own growth. You must find that time spent alone is anything but wasted, indeed is the most profitable way of spending it. In these times alone you can find wisdom and truth derived from meditation and study. All this should help bring peace to your soul and a realization that money and material matters are as nothing set against this inner peace.

Early Development Number 8

With this Early Development Number you will have to learn to gain, handle and use money. Hopefully you will learn to do this without desiring more than is necessary for your needs, and you will realize that money is not everything. The need of the non-material things in life are just as important. It is not only a matter of monetary gain but achieving status and power. Remember, money is not the only way to gain these things. But money and power are significant things which one does well to learn to use in this life in a balanced way.

Early Development Number 9

With this Early Development Number you must learn to give without thought of getting anything back. In other words, it must be unselfish giving, done for the love of it. The giving can take any form, from sympathy to loving care, from money to goods. Know that this can bring the greatest of satisfaction that this life has to offer. Learn to give when it is needed, not when it is wanted.

Early Development Number 11

With this Early Development Number you must learn to develop your intuition. You have to become aware of the world spiritual and become a channel though which others can perceive this as well. Do this by example, but also you must learn to communicate on spiritual matters even though you have many a discouragement. You may have seemed dreamy in youth, on another planet to others. If this has persisted then you must try to come down to earth and make those dreams reality.

Early Development Number 22

With this Early Development Number you must learn to focus your insight at a very high level so that at a later time of life you can work well on significant material and/or spiritual projects. You will develop a strongly practical yet idealistic philosophy with which you will want to bring benefit to other people. This is a very high level growth number and can make life quite hard, especially in younger life because it makes one so very idealistic. Some may have shunned you because of this, but it is likely you have stuck to your guns and in later life will succeed in your projects.

Early Lesson Number

The Early Lesson Number is a challenge given in early life to develop useful characteristics which will help us on the chosen Soul Path later in life. As the name implies, it is something to prod us to seek a valuable lesson for the soul by converting negative energies to positive. An instance might be to overcome shyness or to learn to stand on one's own two feet.

It is one of the only places we find 0 used. We also do not get a 9, 11 or 22 in the charts. The number is reduced in a particular way from our Date of Birth, like this: First reduce each part of the Date of Birth downwards, as before, but do not add them up across. Also reduce 11 and 22, to 2 and 4 respectively.

Here is John's date of birth laid out:

Day: 23	Month: 6	Year: 1946
5	6	20
5	6	2

Now we take the reduced number of the day and the month and subtract the lesser from the greater:

Day = 5

Month = 6

Subtracting the lesser from the greater = 1

Then we take number of the month and the year, and again subtract the lesser from the greater:

Month = 6

Year = 2

Subtracting the lesser from the greater = 4

So, again taking the lesser from the greater of these two numbers: 4 - 1 = 3

So John's Early Lesson Number Chart would look like this:

Date of Birth: Day:……23……/ Month:…….6……/Year:…………1946..

………5……./……………6…………………………20..

………5……./……………6……………………………2..

Day:….5…..Month:…….6……Subtract the lesser from the greater = 1

Month: 6….Year:……2…………Subtract the lesser from the greater = 4

Subtract the lesser from the greater=

the **Early Lesson Number** = 3

Here is the Workout Chart for the Early Lesson Number. Try to work out Jane's number and then your own. (Remember, Jane's date of birth was 1/11/1911.)

Day.......   /   Month.......   /   Year.......
      ....   /   ....   /   ....
      ....   /   ....   /   ....

Subtracting the lesser from the greater:
Day =.......
Month =.......
Then we take number of the month and the year, and again subtract the lesser from the greater:
Month =.......
Year =.......
Now take the lesser from the greater of these two numbers:
.... − .... = ...
Early Lesson Number =.......

Now, Jane's number has some interesting points. You would have had to reduce the 11 to 2, and you should have discovered she has the numerologically unusual Early Lesson Number of 0. Read on and you will discover what this means.

✷
Early Lesson Number Charts

Early Lesson Number 0

Although you could probably recognize and work out solutions to your problems in early life, it is likely that you could not act upon your ideas. You may have made every excuse for this and it could have had a bad effect on your development. The lesson was to teach you to have faith in yourself, and it is hoped it has given you practice at choosing and acting upon your choices in life.

Early Lesson Number 1

In childhood you could have felt that everybody was trying to dominate you, particularly your parents or teachers. You may have felt that your every wish was being thwarted by others and nobody was listening to what you wanted. You would have tried everything to please them, win their approbation, all to no avail. It would have made you more frustrated than ever.

This is the negative of the 1 vibration taken to extreme. It was for you to learn to interact with others without trying to dominate them. You must learn from it and progress in your own direction, taking your own needs into account. In doing so you must not become dominated by others' ideas of what you should do, nor dominate others.

Early Lesson Number 2

In childhood you could have been lacking in self-confidence, been rather put upon by others and given the run around. You would have been compliant due to not wishing to get hurt by the words or actions of others. You may have shunned the company of others even though you wished you could be with them. In other words, in childhood you could have been ultra-sensitive to what others thought about you or said to you.

This is the negative of being sensitive to others' needs, and should have turned to the positive expression of the 2 vibration by adulthood. It can be a tool to bring out intuitive awareness of what another person and their feelings are all about.

Early Lesson Number 3

Although you had creative ability early in life you probably tried to hide it due to shyness and a difficulty to express yourself in public. Lack of social skills will have caused discomfort. You would have probably declined to join in conversations, fearing you were unable to communicate well. This is the negative of 3. It will have taught you to overcome these problems by finding some way of expressing your optimism and joy of living.

Early Lesson Number 4

In childhood and early life you may have found it difficult to get down to hard work. What work was done might have only been accomplished rather ineffectively. You may have hated work and tried to get out of it whenever possible. Or possibly you may have done the work in a rigid way, not really understanding what it would accomplish, doing it because you were told to and not seeing the reason for it. These are the negative sides of the 4 vibration and it may have brought many a retribution down upon your head. This must be turned into a positive attitude by adulthood; it was given to you to teach you to develop an ability to work hard and long with patience, and have an awareness of the reason for the work.

Early Lesson Number 5

Although you probably had many opportunities in your early life, it is likely that you did not take full advantage of them. This would have been due to your rather erratic, impulsive and restless nature. You tired of things easily and wanted to move on. Also, where physical pleasures were concerned it is likely they often got the better of you and limited your potential. The lesson here was intended to teach you to pick the right opportunities and learn to see them through, only moving to new things when the old were accomplished.

Early Lesson Number 6

You probably had difficulties in your young life because you insisted on high standards for yourself and others. You may have been a touch intolerant and self-righteous. No one matched up to your high ideals, or appreciated your work to uplift them. Here you would have been using the 6 vibration, of harmonizing situations and bringing balance, in a negative way. It should have taught you to be more diplomatic and to take time to understand what others need. You must express more universal love and accept others as they are.

Early Lesson Number 7

In your early years your discrimination may have been used in a negative way and caused you to seem aloof, reserved and with a propensity not to express your feelings. Also, you may sometimes have been rather over-critical and complaining. This may have resulted in your being left alone to get on with it. It should have taught you to dispense with this attitude and share your knowledge and wisdom, gained in solitude, with others. It should also have taught you to have faith in your own abilities.

Early Lesson Number 8

While young you may have thought that only material goods were of any importance in life, making them your point of security. You may have done anything to gain material possessions and the status they could bring. This is the negative of this number and you must learn to deal with material things in a sensible manner. Remember the lesson of the number 8 is realizing that there is more beyond this physical, material world.

Remember: there is no Early Lesson Number 9.

Karma and Numerology

If you find the idea of reincarnation difficult, then this side of numerology will not be easy for you. The word Karma has almost become an everyday expression, but few really try to find out just what it means. If they do seek out a meaning they will discover various beliefs, from being reborn as an animal because of a bad past life, to gaining wealth and riches because of an extraordinarily good life, and many other notions in between.

But in numerology we don't really go to these extremes. We work with a more homogenized idea, of some Karma being good, and some, regretfully, not so good. This latter is mostly what we look at here.

First we have what we call a *Karmic Debt*, secondly we have *Karmic Lessons*, with thirdly, a lesser aspect known as *Second Time Karmic Lessons*.

Karmic Debt is just what it says it is – a person has incurred a debt by living in some untoward way. A Karmic Lesson or Second Time Karmic Lesson is something with which we have decided to come to grips and thoroughly learn in the present life. In all three cases, the underlying message is that in former lives we may not have learned all that we should have.

The Karmic Debt is undoubtedly the most important of the three.

Having said this, I would not want you to think that just because you find a Karmic Debt on a chart that the person is wicked or evil. Indeed, the fact that you find such a number on their chart means that somewhere, sometime, they have come to realize that they have done things they wish they had not. They then have chosen this lifetime to put this right – pay off the debt, or at least some of it, either by suffering themselves what they have done to others or by making it up to the very people to whom they caused harm in a former life.

Karmic and Second Time Karmic Lessons are also pointers as to where one went wrong previously. They are lessons administered to make sure you learn either not to do the same things again, or why they were wrong. For, you see, any lesson learned here on earth is much stronger than those learned in the spirit world after death. The unfortunate thing is they are almost always painful.

People with Karmic Debts on their charts, particularly if it is on the Birth Number, often have very difficult and upsetting lives. Things change or are lost without rhyme or reason – one day they have everything, the next nothing. Often they have many upheavals and moves, changes of jobs, and relationships are generally extremely difficult. Enemies come out of nowhere, nothing having been done to cause the enmity.

If the person is coming to grips with these difficult past lives by the age of at least 40, and maybe sooner, they become very strong people. If they do not come to terms with these difficulties then they may be very unhappy, even withdrawn people.

It is here that I feel numerology is of such great help. Either it can serve as a warning, if the reading is done early in life, or it can explain so many things in later life. 'Why do all these things happen to me? – What have I ever done to deserve this?' are the sort of cries heard from people who have a Karmic Debt. I know it can be said of everybody, but if you work out the person's numerology you will often find they have a Karmic Debt number on one of their numbers.

As mentioned before, if a Karmic Debt is found on the Birth Number, then it has great significance on the reading. It must be taken into account and carefully explained. Be very circumspect in how much, and what, you tell the person. If the person has begun to be interested in spiritual matters, then usually they will understand and be glad to know. If it is a chart for someone young then I suggest you keep it to yourself, perhaps just mentioning it to the parent if you think they can understand.

I myself have just such Karmic Debt on my Birth Number, and it was learning about this that has helped me so much. I have really tried to face that debt and the character within me that caused it. I realized that in the first part of my life I was still living in the same way, accruing more debt and not learning from past life experience. Knowing about the debt does not stop difficult things happening, but if you look deeply into your character, admit your faults and try to change, then a kind of peace comes to you which helps you to cope much better with future upheavals.

How to Find Karmic Debt Numbers

So how do we find these numbers? There are only four, which makes them easy to remember. It is here we look at the double number just before we reduce to the final single number. Here are John's and Jane's Birth Number charts again:

```
John:   ......23.......... / ...... 6....... / ...1946
        ..... 5......../ ...... 6....... / .....20
        ..... 5......../ ...... 6....... / ......2
        ..... 5.......+..... 6.......+......2 = _____ 13/4 _____ Birth Number
Jane:   ......1......../ ......11....... / ...1911
        ......1......../ ......11....... / ...12
        ......1......../ ......11....... / ...3
        ......1.......+......11....... +..3 = _____ 15/6 _____ Birth Number
```

From this I can see the John has a Karmic Debt and Jane has not. Why? Because 13 is one of the numbers I am looking for and 15 is not.

The four numbers I look for are: 13/4 – 14/5 – 16/7 – 19/1.

Technically the last has 10 as its last number before its final reduction, but as 0 is not really used it is discounted. Look for the 19. Try to commit these numbers to memory because it is very useful when doing a quick chart for someone whom you know has a rather more troubled life than usual. See how many times these people have one of these numbers in their chart!

Here are the charts for you to understand each Karmic Debt better.

✸

Karmic Debt Charts

Karmic Debt 13/4

This Karmic Debt is brought about by your not getting down to work in past lives, but rather leaving it all up to others, to their detriment. There are things you should have accomplished but didn't. You are likely to have wasted your time frivolously and senselessly. You would have selfishly burdened others without a thought of what you were doing. This will come home to roost in this life in the shape of very hard work with limitations placed on or about you. It will be work for the sake of work rather than what it accomplishes – the work ethic.

If you object to this and try yet again to escape, the problem will be magnified. This magnification may take the form of the negative of this number – rigid, dogmatic and obstinate ways of dealing with life. This will give you more limitations than ever and will lead to endless frustration. You must accept the workload and not look for easy ways out, or people on which to off-load it. Pay attention to the overall view of things as well as the nitty-gritty details in which you can so easily become bogged down.

If you are showing the positive of this number you are likely to be accused of being a workaholic, and this will probably be true. Therefore give some time to watching out for your own health and welfare. Family and relationships can suffer, as you may not give them enough time or thought, thinking that you show your love by working hard to provide the necessities of life for them. Organizing your time, which you should be good at, is the answer here.

Karmic Debt 14/5

A Karmic Debt has come about because of a tendency in past lives to misuse freedom. Probably you will have benefited yourself by the subjection of others to slavery or domination or both. This could have been on a large scale, as a tyrant might dominate and subjugate whole nations, or on a smaller, more personal or family scale which was destructive to the lives of those about you. The 14/5 debt often comes about because of over-involvement in the physical pleasures of the world. To gain these pleasures great wealth is often needed, and gaining this has led to domination of those around you to provide for your needs. These needs would be self-centred and there would have been a lack of accountability.

In this life the 14/5 can show rather more of the negative side of 5 by becoming a rolling stone, never really staying long enough anywhere to actually accomplish the things you set out to do. You never stick with any activity for long, jumping from one thing to another in an erratic manner. A love of the pleasures of life may manifest when quite young, and if left to your own devices without let or hindrance, it can spoil all chances of success. Over-indulgence of all forms – drink, drugs, sex, food – must be watched for and moderated before they have the chance to dominate your life. 14/5s also want continual flow of adrenaline gained from things that are exciting to do. This can be another form of excess. These negatives are extremely dangerous, and in their most exaggerated form can lead to 'Skid Row' and worse.

If you do not come to terms with this debt you will meet with many difficulties in this life. These difficulties will tend to show up in your life as losses and delays that seem inexplicable. 'Why me?' you may ask many times in your life. Now you know, and by knowing bear with them and learn, so that this debt may not have to follow you into future lives. If you continue to be impatient and restless without thought of others, you will only make these difficulties worse.

You must improve things by learning not to repeat mistakes over and over again. Learn from your mistakes and profit by them. You must also curb any appetites that threaten to get out of control. Your watchwords should be 'All things in moderation.' You must also learn the lesson of 'constructive freedom'. Abraham Lincoln was a 5 who was a great example of this expression of freedom, brought to bear on his Emancipation Proclamation granting freedom to the slaves. Freedom does not mean doing anything you want, when you want, and to hell with whether it hurts anyone else. It is having, and allowing others, the freedom you require without any destructive side-effects.

Karmic Debt 16/7

A Karmic Debt has come about because of a tendency in past lives to become involved in love affairs of a doubtful nature – that is, ones that were often unusual, illicit, strange or bizarre. What is sure is that, unfortunately, you did not behave towards your partner in the best way. You could have caused hurt, suffering or shame, and certainly would not have shown responsibility.

This will have left you in this life exhibiting the negative traits of the 7, making you a difficult person to approach – usually because your outward actions disconcert others so they often up and leave you alone. You may also play on your 'differentness' to a point of being awkward. Being a 7, this gets a reaction from you of 'oh well, I want to be alone anyway.' Not true, you like and need loving companionship as much as the next person. Isolation can be taken too far. Yet you will find it difficult to keep relationships of a permanent nature going.

When this debt is found in a Birth Number it can cause much impermanence in life. Things seem to come, but more important they go – with monotonous regularity. Sudden changes happen which can leave you devastated, and which don't seem to happen to other people. Indeed, people will often think there must be something wrong with you, yet you know it was fate at work. Deceptions and losses are common occurrences with this number. Sometimes you are at a loss to know what it is that you have done to deserve this continual reversal of fortune.

What can be done to regain soul balance? Well, quite often you are the cause of your own undoing even if it does seem to be fate. Be honest with yourself and explore this possibility. The greatest way to counteract these trials is to devote your life to loving and serving in selfless ways. Put your own needs last. You must find faith in yourself and accept the changes, using them to grow. If you do not and you exhibit too much pride, things will only get worse. Accept the impermanence and flow with it. Although you may remember nothing of what has led to this debt, it is quite possible that you have, even in this life, continued to act in the same manner, particularly in youth. Now you are seeking to understand yourself and things even greater than yourself. Often the people you hurt in past lives are still around you in your present life, so you never know when you may have the chance to repay your debt by selfless service to others.

Karmic Debt 19/1

This Karmic Debt has come about through the misuse of power over other people in past lives. This means a selfishness that has caused dire results in the lives of others. It means a self-centredness to a point of complete inability to think of the needs of others. Then somewhere along the line has come realization of this fact and a wish to correct and pay off the debt. So in this life there may be signs of the negatives of this number: an inability to relate to the needs of others, and an inability to stand on your own two feet.

The first negative may indeed consist of a complete lack of ability even to see others' needs, let alone acknowledge them. This often brings a negative reaction to your endeavours from others, which you find hard to understand. Other people are thinking 'if there is no thought for me, why should I think of him or her?' The second negative means you will not play 1's leading role, and be dependent on others instead. This can cause much unhappiness, and you will tend to blame others for what is really your own fault, for not thinking positively and getting on with things yourself.

Many difficulties will surface in this life if this debt is not faced. Come to terms with it and look to the needs of others, or work towards independence. Now you know of the debt, it will bring some clarity to the situation. If you have been fighting this and are beginning to see the wood for the trees, you will at least know the 'why' of many difficulties in the past. But the debt's lessons continue the whole of one's life, so things will still come along that need continued strength and purpose. Resolutely express the positive of the number

1, namely, independence, leadership and a pioneering spirit. This must be done without being domineering or egocentric. Nor must you hide in a lazy, selfish personality, or your problems may get worse.

Although a Karmic Debt on the Birth Number is the most important, you will find these numbers on the other numbers in a person's chart. The effect is lessened as the Transformer effect is less. So on the Whole Name Number it is important, the Vowel Number a little less, and Consonant Number even less. The Maturity Number is fairly important, and a Karmic Debt has a strong effect with the Changed Name Number. Other than this, just note its presence, as it does mean there is something here to reckon with.

I feel that if it shows up on numbers other than the Birth Number, the soul has probably begun to have worked this debt out in other lives and has brought the Karmic Debt in either to remind itself or tie up some 'loose ends' not yet worked out.

Some souls can load themselves down with these odds and ends, having several in their chart. I did one chart that had a Karmic Debt on almost every number, including the Birth Number. I asked the person if he was the sort who loaded himself up with many tasks which he thought he was capable of handling yet often failed because he had taken on too much. He agreed that was just what he was like!

During our lives we have come to learn many lessons. To my mind the act of learning is one of the most important things we come to do. In fact, in early life we often have to 'learn to learn'. In numerology there is a way of discovering which lessons we have particularly come to experience – not just once but several times. These are called Karmic Lessons and Second Time Karmic Lessons.

The first is when we have decided to take the lesson for the first time. It is something which we have not yet had a chance to come to grips with, and we have chosen to do so during this life. We choose this, but even so we may try to duck the lesson. For instance, suppose we have an 8 lesson, which means we need to learn to handle money and material goods, and possibly material success. Yet we may ignore this and waste what money comes to us, not learning to conserve and use it wisely. Or perhaps we have had the good fortune to be born into wealth and we misuse it.

A Karmic Lesson is not so much a fault that we have to put right, but more a chance to learn, in depth, the rigours of a particular life lesson. A Second Time

Karmic Lesson is just that – a lesson which you have taken on before in previous lives but which needs just a little more tuition.

Remember, it is through these lessons that we progress. Although they may be hard and painful, they are for our growth. Many are not in the least pleasant; others appear pleasant but have a hidden agenda. To be a slave would be bound to teach us to appreciate freedom (5 lesson), and to be seriously hard working (4 lesson) could bring us security and enough money to be comfortable, but it may cause us to miss out on the fun in life. Address your lessons, if you have not done so already, and be sure you don't need to do them again next time around!

We find the lessons by the expedient of looking at the number in our full name. Set the name out like this:

```
J O H N / D A M I A N / F U L L E R T O N
1     8 5 / 4  1 4 9 1  5 / 6 3 3 3 5 9 2 6  5
```

Now we have to look to see what numbers are missing between 1 – 9.
John has 1, 2, 3, 4, 5, 6, 8, 9 but no 7.
Now we must look at John's other main numbers, which are:

- Birth Number 4
- Whole Name Number 5
- Vowel Number 22
- Consonant Number 1

If a number is missing from all the main numbers as well, then it is a Karmic Lesson Number. If we do find the number elsewhere, then a Second Time Karmic Lesson is in play. In John's case, there is no 7 at all, so John has a Karmic Lesson of 7.

Here is Jane's name set out. Find out what lesson she has:

```
J A N E / R O S E / K I R K B Y
1 1 5 5 / 9 6 1 5 / 2 9 9 2 2 7
```

Here are her other numbers:

- Birth Number 6
- Whole Name Number 1
- Vowel Number 6
- Consonant Number 4

That's right, Jane has two Karmic Lessons and one Second Time Karmic Lesson. Check at the end of this chapter (*page 106*) to see if you got it right.

Now see what lessons you have. Here is a Workout Chart for you to use:

Name _____ / _____ / _____
Nos .... / .... / ....
Numbers present ....
Numbers missing ....
Birth Number ......
Whole Name Number ......
Vowel Number ....
Consonant Number ....
Karmic Lessons ....
Second Time Karmic Lessons ....

★
Karmic Lessons Charts

Karmic Lesson 1

This is the life to learn about gaining independence and confidence. This Karmic Lesson does not often occur, and will have quite a strong effect on your life. Quite often people with this lesson will be not too sure of themselves and not think they are as able as their fellows. It can lead to domination or fear of making decisions, particularly when younger. The whole purpose of this lesson is to learn to stand on your own two feet, so by later life you should have shaken off the negative effects mentioned. Life is apt to be very trying until you do.

Karmic Lesson 2

This is the life to learn consideration for others and sensitivity. You will not have shown much of either in past lives, so this time you have to learn diplomacy if you are going to get on. If you do not then you could face many difficulties until you do learn this lesson. You will also tend to see to the details of things rather than the greater whole.

There is also a lesson about partnership to learn, and how to take a back seat while you let others shine.

Karmic Lesson 3

This is the life to learn to express yourself, although there may be many forces acting against this. One may be the attitude you take in talking to others, which may put them off – you may appear to be aggressive or insensitive of how others are reacting to you. Or you could be withdrawn and appear to lack any confidence in what you are saying. Both these are the negative side of 3. This lesson has come about because you have not bothered to communicate in past lives, nor expressed any joy in living. Improve your general communicating abilities and see the improvement in other people's attitude towards you.

Karmic Lesson 4

This is the life to learn practical organization and hard work. You will not have shown much aptitude for this in past lives, so it will play an important part in this life. If you have 2s, 6s or 8s in your other numbers you will probably be very aware of this already. If you have 1s, 3s, or 5s you will consider the hard work a limitation on the rest of your life. It is better to accept the hard work and learn this lesson thoroughly.

Karmic Lesson 5

This is the life to learn and understand about freedom. You will not have shown any understanding of allowing for change or of freedom in past lives. You are likely to have been intolerant of others and rarely shown much deep interest in them. This lesson is very rare and will have a great effect on your life as a result. You will experience much change and considerable uncertainty in your life, with which you must come to terms by developing versatility. Profit by the experiences in this life and do not avoid the ones that will prove beneficial to you, even though they bring difficulties in their wake.

Karmic Lesson 6

This is the life to learn responsibility and duty. These will be rather thrust upon you, particularly by family. You will not have shown much awareness of responsibility in past lives, so it will play an important part in this life. As you have no other 6s in your main numbers you will find this responsibility particularly irksome. Nevertheless you will learn to have people depend on you and you must also learn to cope all by yourself.

Marriage will take a lot of hard work on your part to succeed, but if you learn balance and service to others it will work.

Karmic Lesson 7

This means that in past lives you have refused to give time or credence to things of what might be called 'an inner nature', or hidden spiritual values. It is a lesson that is very common today in this material world. During this life you may have to face this lesson and begin to find that there is more to life than meets the eye. In doing so you will find the key to your own development and growth – but, unfortunately, it is more than likely that you will choose to ignore this very hard and sometimes rather frightening lesson.

Karmic Lesson 8

This is the life to learn a proper attitude towards money. You will not have shown much awareness of the practical necessities of gaining a living in past lives, so it will play an important part in this life. As you have not got 8s in your important numbers it means you will have to learn to deal with money matters and to make practical judgements. If you continue with this lack of awareness life will present you with curbs that force you take things seriously. No great satisfaction will come until you do.

Karmic Lesson 9

This lesson is not often encountered, but it means that you have to learn to give without thought of self. You may find this difficult while young and in the negative of this number, but life will keep bringing you trials until you accept the lesson of humanitarian giving.

Start close to home and widen your circle of helpfulness until you find this lesson quite easy and rewarding in an inner way.

Second Time Karmic Lessons Charts

Second Time Karmic Lesson 1

This means you may lack self-confidence and have difficulty in standing up for your own rights. Because you have a 1 in your other numbers you may be well aware of this already. If these difficulties are to end, then stop trying to make excuses for yourself or rationalizing. Learn to be independent and find good motivation to achieve your ambitions.

Second Time Karmic Lesson 2

If you haven't learned sensitivity and diplomacy from your other 2s, then you need to have a look at why this side of your personality has not developed. Things to do with partnership may also be brought to the fore in your life.

Second Time Karmic Lesson 3

There may be some difficulties with expressing yourself in your social encounters. You may not be too good at putting yourself over to others. You must work hard on expressing your feelings and building confidence in your ability to express yourself. Make the 3s in your other numbers work for you.

Second Time Karmic Lesson 4

This means that for you to finish anything calls for great attention to nitty-gritty detail. Because you have a 4 in your other numbers you are probably well aware of this already. With hard work and practical organization you can get through even if there seem to be limitations put on you.

Second Time Karmic Lesson 5

As you have a 5 in your numbers you will probably be fairly aware already that freedom is an important issue in your life. This lesson sometimes causes lack of adaptability, limiting understanding because you fail to learn from life's lessons. It can make you stay with relationships and situations when, in truth, they are worn out.

Second Time Karmic Lesson 6

Family ties will play an important role in your life. You will be into parenting and family responsibilities, which you should shoulder willingly. Here also you must show balance and service to others. These others will depend on you to keep things going. This lesson is to teach you how to cope in group situations and be there when you are needed.

Second Time Karmic Lesson 7

This means that in this life you will come to appreciate things unseen as well as seen. There can be a realization that the non-material world is just as real as the material, and lead to you having longer-lasting values. Indeed, spiritual values will mean more to you as life goes on, and can finally bring deep joy and peace.

Second Time Karmic Lesson 8

You may be slightly out of balance in the way you approach money in your life. This may cause problems in other areas of your life. Because you have an 8 in your other numbers you will probably be aware of this already. You must learn how to deal with money and/or dependence on others, which is difficult for you.

Second Time Karmic Lesson 9

This lesson can cause you to have emotional difficulties until you learn to be more generous with your time and goods. The negative of 9 is keeping hold of things rather than giving them to those in need; move to the positive.

The answer to Jane's numbers was:

> Numbers present: 1, 2, 5, 6, 7, 9
> Karmic Lessons: 3, 8
> Second Time Karmic Lessons: 4

Missing and Repeated Numbers

Here are additional ways of discovering traits about ourselves and others through numerology.

Missing numbers reveal information through what is *not* there rather than what is. We take all the reduced numbers from 1 to 9 (11 and 22 are reduced to 2 and 4) and see what is missing. These missing numbers show areas of endeavour to develop in your life. Sometimes they may seem a little contradictory, such as that you should develop individuality *and* partnership. But we all have to do a bit of both in our lives.

These numbers are minor energies in charts.

Let's take Jane's numbers:

- Birth Number: 6
- Whole Name Number: 8
- Vowel Number: 1
- Consonant Number: 7
- Maturity Number: 7

Missing Numbers: 2, 3, 4, 5, 9

Here are John's numbers again:

- Birth Number: 4
- Whole Name Number: 5
- Vowel Number: 22/4
- Consonant Number: 1
- Maturity Number: 1

Which ones are missing? (Answers at the end of this section – *page 109.*)
Now find your missing numbers and see what they mean.

✳

Missing Numbers Charts

Missing Number 1

Be much more assertive. Make people sit down and listen to what you are saying. Take control and lead the way more. Dare to live to the full. Pick one thing to start with and seek excellence. With confidence gained, move on to full control of self and others.

Missing Number 2

You are possibly being too much of an individual and not co-operating too well with others. Team work is important, so try to show more sympathy and tolerance. Sometimes in life one must take a back seat and let others shine.

Missing Number 3

How can people understand you if you don't communicate your feelings to them? Practise this communication more. Be more happy and cheerful, sourpusses never do well. Watch how you turn yourself out each day; give a good impression of yourself.

Missing Number 4

Is discipline a little lacking here? Build yourself some strong foundations and bring a bit of order into your life. It will benefit any task you have to tackle. Learn to handle your money better as well, then everything should go more smoothly.

Missing Number 5

Get out and about, there's a great big wonderful world out there for you to explore. Ruts are very boring anyway. Go and see what you are missing. More adaptability is needed, which will help you fit in better with others and not seem a stick in the mud.

Missing Number 6

Possibly you are not taking your family responsibilities seriously enough. They need your love and support. Actually tell and show them how you feel about them more often. Think a little bit more about others and a little less of yourself.

Missing Number 7

Give some time to your inner and more intellectual and spiritual needs. Find time to be alone with your thoughts, ponder more on the meaning of life. Broadening your view of life is always worthwhile and brings a little peace into your world.

Missing Number 8

A bit more hard work and effort plus some good business sense might help to push you up the ladder. Without them you will always be a middle-man or -woman. The world could be your oyster if only you would stick it out and overcome difficulties.

Missing Number 9

Philanthropy is not just a long word, it means the world does need your help. Your example may make others care as well, so start caring and sharing. Don't live with tunnel vision, you could be much more expansive if you tried.

John's missing numbers were 2, 3, 6, 7, 8, 9

Repeated Numbers

More information can be gained by examining the repeated numbers within the Date of Birth.

So, with John's date of birth of 23/6/1946 we have:

1   1

2   1

3   1

4   1
5   0
6   2
7   0
8   0
9   1

Jane's Date of Birth was 1/11/1911. Work out her Repeated Numbers:

1   …
2   …
3   …
4   …
5   …
6   …
7   …
8   …
9   …

Jane really has an unusual Date of Birth, hasn't she? Now work out your own Repeated Numbers.

These Repeated Number charts are a little more light-hearted than the rest. We can't be so serious all the time!

✶
Repeated Numbers Charts

One 1

Sometimes you may be thought not to care and to be cool, due to an inability to show your deeper feelings.

Two 1s

You are able to put things into words easily, and your way of looking at life is well balanced.

Three 1s

Very talkative but always interesting, never dull. Into a lot of activities and good to be with.

Four 1s

Often hurt because of a shy nature. Uncommunicative about self because of very deep feelings.

Five 1s or more

Will sometimes become hermit-like because of great difficulty in relating to other people. Can become unstable.

One 2

Not good when in competition with others. Do not like criticism and easily hurt.

Two 2s

Your first thoughts about anybody are usually right because your perception is good.

Three 2s

Because of the wall you build about yourself for protection some people think you are insensitive.

Four 2s

Watch that sarcastic tongue or even ill temper. Reacting too quickly or too much can make a bad situation worse.

Five 2s or more

You may be having a life of bitter disillusionment, and may be feeling very hard done by.

One 3

Alert, intelligent and noted for your long and retentive memory.

Two 3s

Put that over-active imagination to good use or will find it all wasted in daydreams.

Three 3s

Too long on your own thinking and thinking could alienate you from those whom you love and care for.

Four 3s

Imagination run riot can cause confusion. Sometimes there is too much mental activity.

One 4

Happiest when doing and making, not thinking. Very good with your hands.

Two 4s

A bit more fantasy is needed in your life. Take time out from physical occupations to just think.

Three 4s

Usually prefer hard manual work. Not given to thinking, you live for your work.

Four 4s

Beware, damage to the body by physical over-work can happen.

One 5

Your character has great depths. Your self-control is strong.

Two 5s

Although usually in balance and confident, be careful this confidence is not over done. Some difficulty with emotive situations.

Three 5s

Given to speaking without thinking first, which can cause pain.

Four 5s

'Out of the frying pan into the fire' type people. Beware, it's you who suffers.

One 6

Nest-makers. Born to make a happy atmosphere in the home.

Two 6s

Over-love of home. Beware of getting too house-proud – home is a place to relax.

Three 6s

Over-protective of that which they love. Often live in disorder and disarray.

Four 6s

Very rare! A likely genius, with all the emotional problems that goes with it.

One 7

The only way to gain wisdom is by suffering a little.

Two 7s

Sacrifices on all fronts called for if life's lessons are to be learned.

Three 7s

Will pay dearly for the gift of understanding life's ways. A hard way to learn.

Four 7s

The knocks of your life will need the development of enormous strength of character if you are to survive.

One 8

Stay positive and you won't stagnate mentally. You pay great attention to detail and are very neat and tidy.

Two 8s

So good at summing up people it's uncanny, and not always liked. Good with your work but subject to over-confidence at times.

Three 8s

Unlikely to settle to their life's vocation in youth. Matures late, when everything has been tried.

Four 8s

The emotional travellers of life, skipping here and there. This often means they miss the emotional boat/train/plane.

One 9

What you've got is good! Nothing in life is perfect.

Two 9s

Not likely to see the funny side of life. Your own high standards can make you very critical of others.

Three 9s

If bad-tempered and unpredictable it could be your struggle for utmost perfection that is the cause. Learn when and where to let things go.

Four 9s

Nothing is ever right! Nobody and nothing pleases. Tend to be withdrawn.

Numerology Grids

Now we come to the last of the personal traits found in our numerology numbers. There are others, but they are for you to research and find for yourself. I have stayed with those that are basic and fairly easy to discover.

Grids can be worked out on both the Date of Birth and the First Name Numbers. Sometimes these grids are called Pythagorean Arrows. Pythagoras, who live 500 years before Christ, is thought of as the father of Western Numerology. The following is thought to be one of his methods.

First we draw a Noughts-and-Crosses type of grid and place the numbers in it, as shown in Figure 7:

3	6	9
2	5	8
1	4	7

Figure 7

Then we will take John's Date of Birth, which was 23/6/1946, and place the numbers according to the grid shown in Figure 8:

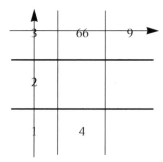

Figure 8

Study the Grid below and then apply the direction of the arrows according to whether the squares have numbers in or are empty. Look above at John's Grid. He has only two complete lines – 3-6-9 and 1-2-3 – yet no arrow-direction is completely empty. Now, with Jane's strange Date of Birth, 1/11/1911, there are many empty squares and no complete lines at all (see Figure 9).

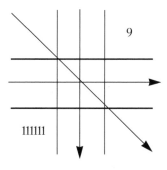

Figure 9

Each arrow is numbered in Figure 10, below, according to the domain over which they hold sway. If the numbers of a person's Date of Birth or First name fall into any of the quadrants along an arrow's course, it is termed Positive; if the quadrants it crosses are empty, it is considered Negative.

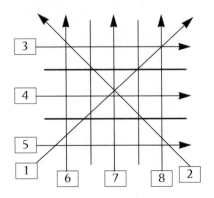

Figure 10

Draw a grid and practise with your Date of Birth and with others.

Now we do exactly the same with first names.

Draw grids and practise, first with John's name (below), and then with your own and others.

```
J O H N
1 6 8 5
J A N E
1 1 5 5
```

Poor Jane, two more Negatives and still no Positives, and John, well I hope you worked out his before I tell you that the placement of his numbers makes it impossible for there to be any arrows at all.

The Grid charts below explain the meanings for the different possibilities. They work for both First Names and Dates of Birth.

Please note that the numbers do not use their numerological meanings – the reading comes from the position of the arrows on the Grids.

I would also like to say, do not think these meaning are set in stone. Quite often they conflict with each other, one saying one thing, the other quite the opposite, thereby almost cancelling each other out. Also, see if a weakness of one chart (say, for the Date of Birth) is offset by the arrows in the other, or, possibly, strengthened.

✷
Grid Charts

Grid 1: Possessing 1-5-9 (Positive Characteristics)

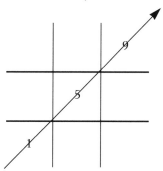

Strong and continued intentions. Great purpose and patience in all you do. Able to concentrate and show persistence and determination. Showing devotion.

Grid 1A: Missing 1-5-9 (Negative Characteristics)

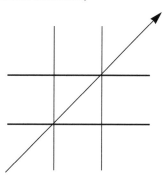

Not very willing. Hesitation and indecision are shown here. A reluctance to do anything. Unable to resolve things easily and disinclined to try.

Grid 2: Possessing 3-5-7 (Positive Characteristics)

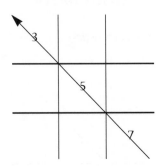

Aware of Higher Self. Great insight into the inner self, combined with a sound philosophy of life. Understanding of consciousness and the perceptions of the mind.

Grid 2A: Missing 3-5-7 (Negative Characteristics)

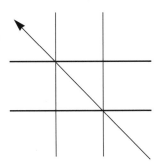

Things metaphysical are not trusted. Understanding of human nature could be better. A large streak of scepticism here, loss of faith, distrust and suspicion.

Grid 3: Possessing 3-6-9 (Positive Characteristics)

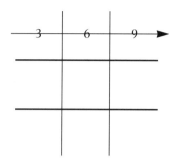

Intellect is first here, a good mind with reasoning paramount. Can grasp concep-tions, has understanding, can discriminate and make judgements.

Grid 3A: Missing 3-6-9 (Negative Characteristics)

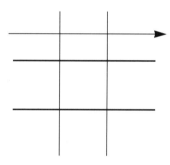

Mental faculties may not be used to best advantage. Likely to find life rather dreary. Beware forgetfulness and absent-mindedness as a result of not having a terribly good memory.

Grid 4: Possessing 2-5-8 (Positive Characteristics)

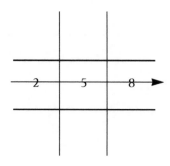

Very even-tempered; able to get things in proportion. Nice sense of balance here and a lot of harmony of the emotions. Keeps things running easily and smoothly.

Grid 4A: Missing 2-5-8 (Negative Characteristics)

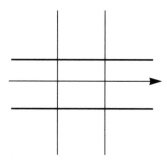

A bit of thin-skinned touchiness here. Likely to get over-emotional and thereby easily hurt. Could be due to feelings of inferiority and inadequacy. Over-sensitive.

Grid 5: Possessing 1-4-7 (Positive Characteristics)

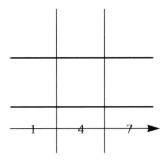

'Actions speak louder than words' is the motto here. Very good with the hands, capable of making things rather than theorizing about them. Very practical.

Grid 5A: Missing 1-4-7 (Negative Characteristics)

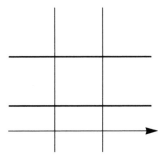

Everything happens at random here, left to chance. A casual air about life, nothing done by design, all unplanned. Uncertainty and unpredictability are the keywords.

Grid 6: Possessing 1 2 3 (Positive Characteristics)

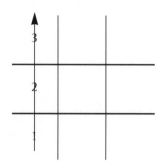

A love of keeping things in order. Wonderful at collating anything, making arrangements or planning, administering an organization or thinking up a new method for doing things.

Grid 6A: Missing 1-2-3 (Negative Characteristics)

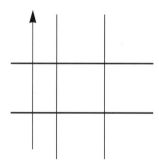

Chaos can reign here with a vengeance. Everything in disarray, likely to be messy and uncoordinated. Keeping things in a muddle makes life very complicated – find a bit of order!

Grid 7: Possessing 4-5-6 (Positive Characteristics)

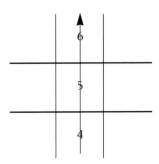

Likely to have hopes and dreams, and the strength to make them come true. A need to possess here and likely to have wants and needs, even cravings for things that give pleasure, sometimes for the self but also for others.

Grid 7A: Missing 4-5-6 (Negative Characteristics)

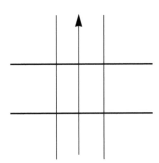

Hopes may have been dashed here; great disappointments and disillusionment likely. Nothing is up to expectations – feelings of rejection, defeat and regret can cloud life.

Grid 8: Possessing 7 8 9 (Positive Characteristics)

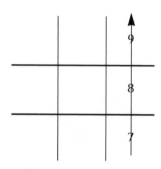

What energy here – finding a great many things to do and doing them with enthusiasm and enterprise. Industriousness is the watch word, always active and eager to participate in everything.

Grid 8A: Missing 7-8-9 (Negative Characteristics)

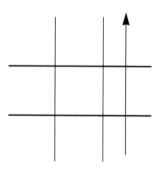

Apathy leads to inaction and sheer sloth. Passive submission to life leaves a feeling of 'why bother at all?' Likely to lie about idle, languid and lifeless. In fact, all life can go dormant.

Please Note

If there are NO possible Grids in Date of Birth Number or Name Number: This is good and means lessons have been learned and traits have been balanced out over past lives.

part two

Other Numbers, Other Secrets Revealed

We have come to the end of looking at the personal traits and soul meanings of the numbers found in our Date of Birth and Name. If you make a chart up from all the forgoing methods, a surprising amount of information can be gathered. (You will find a complete Workout Chart at the back of this book which you can photocopy or use as a basis for your own Workout Charts.)

Some numerologists use numerology to foretell the trends of the future or to give people 'Lucky numbers'. I do not feel that numerology is much use in actually foretelling what will happen, but it does indicate trends.

Personal Year Number

Every year has its own Number, gained by the simple expedient of adding the numbers across, for example: 1947 = 1 + 9 + 4 + 7 = 21 = 2 + 1 = 3, and 1999 = 1 + 9 + 9 + 9 = 28 = 2 + 8 = 10 = 1. Everyone looks at the year 2000, or 2001, as being the beginning of something special. But in numerology the new circle 1 – 9 begins with the last year of the old millennium.

Each year, then, possesses the energies of its number according to the meanings we have come to know so well by now, 1 a year of individuality, 5 a year of freedom, 7 an introspective and mystical year, etc. This energy does not really impinge on us individually very much. It is more of a background energy.

Things are different when we come to our own Personal Year. This can have quite an effect on our day-to-day activities.

By 'Personal Year' I mean a number which relates to you during a given year – you will experience the energies of this number as the year progresses.

Each Personal Year starts on your birthday and runs until your next. But please note that during the first three months after your birthday you will still be under the influence of the previous Personal Year Number to some extent; similarly, during the three months leading up to your next birthday (and next Personal Year) there is a foreshadowing of the next number.

We find our own personal year by using the Day and the Month of our Date of Birth plus the present year.

As an example, here is Jane's Personal Year worked out.

Day ....1........... / Month.......11.......... / Present Year...1998...
..........1.......... /............... 11.......... / ....27......
..........1.......... /............... 11.......... / ....9.......=..21..=..3

Personal Year

Now I know this makes Jane out to be a very old lady, but she is the same age as my own mother, who at the time of writing is more hale and hearty than myself. In fact it is most interesting to do a chart for an older person, because they have their whole life to look back on, and this can help you to ascertain if your synthesizing is correct. Sometimes they say 'Oh, that's not me', but this is mainly because, if they have been wise, they have worked from the negative to the positive of their numbers. Or, unfortunately, stayed in the negative, failing to learn from their life's experience.

So Jane would be in a 3 year in 1998, which would mean it's a good year to go out and communicate to others all her wonderful experience of life.

In giving these chart readings, please emphasize that this is not something that is definitely going to happen, just a trend – to help you learn to go with the flow.

Here is an empty Workout Chart, so that you can work out your own Personal Year.

Day .... / Month................... / Present Year............
.... /........................... / ....
.... /........................... / ....=...../.....

Personal Year

✱

Personal Year Charts

Year Read-out 1

You start a new cycle this year (1 – 9). Time to get away from the old and start new things. Make a break from any energy-demanding situation that is draining you. Money flow could improve this year, with an emphasis on property deals.

This year will decide the tenor of the next nine years, so this is the time to make changes and start new ventures. Instigate some of those plans you made last year. Start as you mean to go on. It may well be the time to go it alone in business, for 1 stands for individuality.

Year Read-out 2

Changes are not a good idea this year; consolidate what was started last year. Wait for things to come to you – if you push you might lose all you have gained. Work on co-operation, the watch-word of 2.

Think about your weak points and your strengths and realize how others view you. There can be emotionally upsetting times this year which could bring disharmony in their wake. Learn self-control if you want to hide your feelings of insecurity. Be prepared for delays and frustrations this year.

Year Read-out 3

A year when your mental capacity and intellect really get going. A good year for enrolling in further study or skill-improving courses. Still not a year to contemplate changes, but it can be a fun year. Romance is likely.

Don't waste your energies on emotional upsets; learn to handle them constructively. And don't let self-indulgence pull down the progress you have made or stop you enjoying the pleasures of a 3 year. Self-improvement is the key word for this year, and expression of the joy of living.

Year Read-out 4

A year for recharging the batteries. Watch after your personal health, mental and physical. Try not to make large changes in your life, as they may not be too successful. Give yourself a chance to rest and recuperate.

Work on making a stable base from which to develop your future. Organize and get ready to expand your horizons when the chance appears.

Don't neglect work altogether; make sure your obligations are met – but certainly relieve the pressure with a little fun.

Year Read-out 5

Midway point on the cycle of 1 – 9 years. Check through what you have learned in the last four years and start to reawaken the artistic part of yourself.

If you live in a city or town, a change to the countryside might work out well. If not a move, then break away from old routines and find something to do that is really new and progressive.

In fact a change might come of its own accord this year, so watch out for good chances. But don't get restless – impulsiveness might cut down your chances of success.

Year Read-out 6

6 represents the family and responsibility. A very good year to marry, work on your marriage or concentrate on the loving joy of any relationship. Business partnerships could do well and be profitable. This is a year to create a beautiful atmosphere around yourself. Expand the artistic pursuits begun last year. Movement is happening in your life, even if it isn't noticeable. Things outside the home go very slowly, but the harmony you engender in the home will make up for this, with many demands on your time.

Year Read-out 7

Introspection is the name of the game in a 7 year. Time to attend to the inward person. Take time to contemplate just what this world, and maybe the next, is all about. Others might find you a bit withdrawn this year, but you are just preparing the way for next year, clearing the decks and laying down the ground-work for possible business expansion.

Meanwhile develop your own inner faith in yourself and an awareness of higher things. Put yourself through a health-check.

Year Read-out 8

This is the year when it should all come together. 8 stands for material success and gain. All those plans and ventures started in year 1 should now bear fruit, especially if you have worked hard. If there is any year in which you should accomplish what you set out to do, it's this year.

There will be opportunities galore for advancement on all fronts, and you should have the energy to make the most of them. This is not the time to dream but the time to act practically, using all your gathered knowledge.

Year Read-out 9

9 marks the end of the cycle. It is a time when you complete many things. Now is the time to sort out what you want to take forward into year 1 of your new cycle next year. Old relationships which are worn out, business ties that are not working, let them go. Yes, there could be big changes in your life this year.

This is the year to plan new beginnings, but not a year to make them. Not a good year to marry, but you can prepare for it in the last few months in the overlap of cycles.

Compatibility

The penultimate work I will give you usually interests everyone. 'Are my partner and I truly compatible?' is something that is frequently asked of me. We covered something similar in Conflict and Harmony, but that was within our own numbers. It is a little different when it comes to whether two people will get on well together, or discovering why they don't! This is a very useful tool in helping people with their partnership problems, be they personal, business or just day-to-day interactions.

We use the Birth Number of the two people.

In giving out these Read-outs, never say to people that they definitely will or won't get on together, for they may be – as my husband and myself – the very worst ratings for compatibility, yet work very well together (we celebrated our silver wedding anniversary in 1996). So don't panic!

Nor should you rely entirely on these charts, they are only to be used as a guide. What has to be pointed out is the needs of the partner and how to accommodate these needs. 7 needs to have time alone and, if married to a 2 who wants constantly to be with their partner, this can cause friction. With knowledge can come understanding. Anybody seeking a spiritual reading will usually understand this only too well.

We do these charts by ratings of how many stars are given: 1* 2** 3*** or 4****. The more stars, the better the rating. I provide a Business Rating and a Personal Partnership Rating. As with the Conflict and Harmony charts, I do not repeat, say, a 7–1 when 1–7 has already been covered (the rating will be the same either way; if you do not find it under one, look under the other). Nor have I given 11 or 22 – you must reduce these numbers to 2 and 4. Of course you can take into consideration the fact of the Master Number being present if you are giving a reading, but as the person may not always be using their full Master Number potential all the time it will be difficult to give an exact compatibility rating. Generally I would say Master Numbers add some friction to a partnership because of the nervous tension in the person with the Master Number.

★
Compatibility Charts

Remember, you use the Birth Number of each person.

1 with 1

Business ***
Personal ***
Both being the same is not easy, but for 1s it is not too bad. Don't let a sense of rivalry emerge – remember you are both on the same side so you should have the same goals. You must co-operate with each other and possibly define areas of leadership. Give each other space to be individual.

1 with 2

Business: ****
Personal: ****
Wonderful in every way. The 2 will keep the partnership together, as that is their forte, and the 1 will have brilliant ideas which the 2 will know just how to work out. Each of you should have the talents, etc. the other lacks, so together you make a splendid combination, unbeatable and unstoppable.

1 with 3

Business: ***
Personal: **
A very rewarding partnership if it is understood that the 1 usually leads the way. 3 will brighten all they do and use all of 1's ideas to the full. 1 must be careful not to do anything too rash, and 3 must keep their mind on the job in hand, then all should go quite well indeed.

1 with 4

Business: ***
Personal: *
4s are not in the least impulsive, which is not something that can be said of 1s. A great deal of understanding is needed here for a personal relationship to prosper. Not such a bad thing in business, as the 1 can get cautious old 4 out of a rut and careful 4 can put the breaks on 1 when necessary.

1 with 5

Business: ***
Personal: **
Both of you change horses often and easily. Each of you must be ready to change and change again for each other, adapting and coping all the time. But you are both very versatile, so it should work out, particularly in business, less so in personal matters.

1 with 6

Business: ***
Personal: ***
1 is very good at providing the good things in life, which 6 enjoys, so this is a fine start to a personal relationship. 1 must always give 6 plenty of time and space to be creative. Quite good in business, as both have different areas they can cover and 1 is a good manager.

1 with 7

Business: **
Personal: **
Can be an bit of an odd partnership – 7 tends to turn inwards while 1 is outgoing. Still, if there is give and take then 1 can carry through some of 7s good ideas, and 7 will stop 1 acting without thinking enough first. 1 must not forget 7 has to be alone at times; it's not that they 'don't want you'.

1 with 8

Business: ****
Personal: ****/*

It's everything or nothing with this combination. Both of you are excellent at business and could make an unstoppable partnership. Might be an idea to give each other well-defined zones of operation, though. On a personal level there has to be an enormous amount of give and take for this to work, but it is very rewarding if this is done.

1 with 9

Business: ****
Personal: ****

Together you have that certain touch that should make anything zing with success, be it business or personal. 9's wise ways will help 1 with their bright ideas by giving sympathetic listening time, and 1 has the business get-up-and-go. Terrific in every way.

2 with 2

Business: **
Personal: ****

Wonderful: you both like partnership better than being individuals. Be a little watchful that you give each other the chance of doing the caring bit. Receive as well as give, especially in business. One or both of you will have to learn to make decisions, as this does not come too easily to either of you.

2 with 3

Business: **
Personal: ***

Should be friendly because 2 likes to make partnerships work and 3 is the one to make things work with their terrific communication skills. 2 may have to take a back seat sometimes while 3 is busy communicating with everyone. This is fine, though, as 2 likes to give happiness to others and will like seeing 3 enjoy themselves.

2 with 4

Business: ***
Personal: ***
Pleasant and harmonious is the description of this partnership's possibilities. 4 likes to build a business or a home, and 2 likes to keep it ticking over. You really should go together very well.

2 with 5

Business: *
Personal: *
There will have to be a lot of give and take and even more hard work to keep this combination alive. 5s like change and travel, and 2s tend to stay put. 5s will tend to lose interest quickly in the 2, who will seem rather staid. 2 may always be wondering where 5 has got to. Business together has not really got good possibilities.

2 with 6

Business: *
Personal: ***
Better for personal relationships than business here. Both 2 and 6 are real home-lovers – 2 will make it comfortable while 6 will make it utterly beautiful using their artistic abilities. But in business neither has the get-up-and-go to make it really successful.

2 with 7

Business: *
Personal: ***
On a personal footing these two will be so peaceful you would think heaven had broken out here on earth, but this is not too good a partnership in business unless it is something in the esoteric line such as a healing or meditation centre. This partnership can be on a very high spiritual level.

2 with 8

Business: ***
Personal: ***
This partnership can do very well as both are industrious and 2 will keep the partnership going, as they don't like to be alone. 8 will probably be the more dynamic of the two and must try not to outdo 2 too often. Altogether a pleasant and harmonious relationship can be had from this combination.

2 with 9

Business: ****
Personal: ****
Here is a pair that could help put the world to rights together. A lovely combination – 9 with a giving nature and breath of imagination, and 2 who is giving in partnership, has wonderful understanding, and forms stable foundations for anything done together.

3 with 3

Business: *
Personal: *
Regretfully this is not a good combination, as you both tend to leave everything to luck and gamble your chances away on all sides. With no break on this tendency things can go from bad to worse. It would take considerable work to hold this partnership together and you would both have to learn to be more responsible.

3 with 4

Business: **
Personal: **
Quite a lot of work to make this partnership successful, but it is possible if 4 can cope with 3's incautious attitude to life and if 3 can put up with 4's almost excessive caution. This being sorted out, it can be quite a good combination. 4 must listen to 3's clever thoughts and not always be so busy.

3 with 5

Business: ***
Personal: **
Beware of both being too hasty in your decisions and things won't be too bad.
You can have many bright ideas between you, and then 5 will know how to make
the best out of what 3 has turned into an attractive package. Both of you are
outward going and you can travel happily together along life's road.

3 with 6

Business: ***
Personal: ***
This is one of those partnerships that once put together nothing puts asunder,
you have decided it's time to settle down and grow roots. 6s love home life and
make good marriage partners. In business you could have a very solid partnership. 3s should be the ones to communicate to outsiders.

3 with 7

Business: ***
Personal: ***
This can be a rewarding combination if you give each other space. This is particularly so in 7s case, as they need time to themselves more than any other number.
3 is bright with energy and can gain wisdom from 7s deep thoughts. 7 gets new
ideas from 3 to ponder on.

3 with 8

Business: ****
Personal: **
Excellent for a business combination as you both have such grand schemes
going round in your heads. Not so good on the personal level. 8 should let 3 be the
public relations officer or salesperson of the two, for 3 can communicate
anything to others. 8 is the business head of the two. Do try to aim for the same
thing if you want to be successful.

3 with 9

Business: *
Personal: ****

Regretfully, in business neither of you is likely to get any work actually done! Even in personal matters you are better when there is no responsibility needed. If there is plenty of money to support you both you couldn't find a better partner to discover the world and enjoy it with.

4 with 4

Business: ****
Personal: ***

With two 'builders' like this any business can be a success, and personal partnerships can also flourish. You could be the envy of all for the material success you gather around you, so be a little careful that you don't forget the other things that make life worthwhile.

4 with 5

Business: **
Personal: **

Despite outward appearances of these being opposites it can work if both parties adjust. 5 will do most of the latter, while 4 offers practicality. Of all opposites this combination has the best chance of success after much effort has gone into the partnership.

4 with 6

Business: ***
Personal: ***

A good solid partnership can be had from this combination. You both could feel very fulfilled and happy with this relationship. In business you might do best if you go for an entertainment, leisure or advertising industry. 4 will build while 6 will sustain.

4 with 7

Business: ****
Personal: ****

In this combination 7s can rely on the good foundation built by 4, and 4 can enjoy the brilliant insights 7 can provide. It really can be the best of both worlds, 4 the material and 7 the spiritual nurture needed by all to cope with tribulations and trials. A good balance here.

4 with 8

Business: ****
Personal: ***

A good balance here for both personal and business although business has the edge. This is because 8s are the businesspeople of the world and see things on a grand scale. Fours will steadily build the foundations and sees to minutiae that 8s often miss. Don't become too materialistic, life has much else to offer.

4 with 9

Business: **
Personal: ***

This combination is really better in personal relationships than business. While 4 builds and builds, 9 might be busy giving it away to the needy. 4 must teach 9 to be more practical and conserve energies. 9 must show 4 the humanitarian side of life and impart their wisdom and love for all.

5 with 5

Business: *
Personal: *

One to be missed if at all possible. If already entered upon then you must come to terms with living in a continually explosive and difficult situation. Both have restless energy and a need for constant change. The restrictions of relationships are difficult as you both want freedom. Definitely not easy.

5 with 6

Business: **
Personal: ***

6's love of home and family brings the better chance of success in personal partnerships, as this steadies 5 down a bit. 5 will help 6 get out and about to see the world. 5 might change radically while under the influence of 6, but 6 must not leave 5 without any freedom or they may regret it.

5 with 7

Business: *
Personal: *

5 is unlikely to leave 7 the space to find inner peace, and 7 will not want to do all the rushing around that 5 indulges in. Not a good start for any relationship. 7 will become unstabilized and 5 will be frustrated. If the partnership has existed for some time then there has been a lot of give and take on both sides.

5 with 8

Business: ****
Personal: ****

Great! 5 has wonderful ideas and 8 can use them to print money. The pace is fast and furious, but sometimes can go too fast unless someone can step on the brakes. The end of the relationship can happen from this burn-out, so learn to slow down a little and enjoy what you have together.

5 with 9

Business: ***
Personal: ***

9 is wise in their ways with a lot of knowledge which 5 knows just how to get over to others – for 5 could sell anything. On the other side of the coin, 9 knows just what to say and do to get the very best out of 5's abilities, and yet will have seemed to do absolutely nothing. Clever old 9.

6 with 6

Business: *
Personal: ****
Now, if you're thinking of going in for interior decor as a business, fine – but anything else might not do so well. The reason is that both 6s are tied up with home considerations, making the home beautiful and comfortable for each other. A weekend decorating together is bliss. What a lovely home you'll have.

6 with 7

Business: *
Personal: *
Unfortunately a very difficult combination. 6 is locked into home and material considerations, and 7s thoughts are rather immaterial and unworldly, not really caring too much about their surroundings. 7 must come down to earth occasionally and notice 6's hard work, and 6 must give 7 vast amounts of space and free time.

6 with 8

Business: ***
Personal: ****
Really quite a good mixture, as 8 generally is the leader and 6 does not mind as they like creating a comfortable atmosphere for work or home. 8 will bring home the money which 6 will turn into a beautiful home. Each knows which part to play and is happy to play it.

6 with 9

Business: ***
Personal: ****
Lovely mix of numbers here – 9 has knowledge, wisdom and truth with a supremely giving nature, and 6 loves beauty and finds pleasure in making and giving it to others. 6 is in touch with giving on a small scale, 9 in touch with universal giving. Make sure you keep enough to live on yourselves.

7 with 7

Business: *
Personal: ****

Blissful – 7 being the only other one who can understand another 7. With both of you somewhat out of this world, business together could be a disaster. Even your own material needs will suffer if you don't come down to earth. Ideas alone will not feed you, but what beautiful music of the spheres you listen to together.

7 with 8

Business: ****
Personal: ***

Excellent – 7 can pierce the gloom of the hidden future with their intuition, which helps with planning, and 8 provides the worldly business sense. 8 must be careful not to try to dominate 7 and must leave them time and space enough to dream up ideas. 7s must get 8 to use their energy to the best advantage.

7 with 9

Business: **
Personal: ****

Lovely combination, but be careful that you are not so heavenly that you are no earthly good. You are both so likely to be into things of a spiritual nature that only a humanitarian-type business – such as a therapy or esoteric centre – has a chance of success. In personal relationships it should be harmony all the way.

8 with 8

Business: */****
Personal: */****

Brilliant success or dreadful disaster, either could be true of this combination. 8s have the possibility of co-operating and making them an unbeatable team, or fighting each other and destroying everything. Give each other well-defined roles in business and personal life. Make sure it is brilliant success.

8 with 9

Business: **
Personal: ***
8 might get rather tired of 9's humanity to all as they give away all that 8 has worked so hard to get. Probably the best combination for an 8 so that they may learn the lesson of their number, the illusion of materiality. But the combination can work quite well as they bring out the best qualities in each other.

9 with 9

Business: **
Personal: ****
A well-matched pair who will demonstrate the gift of giving with imagination, wisdom and love. They could bring great humanitarian benefit to all the world. Don't over-extend yourselves at the same time, then each can care for the other's likely exhaustion in turn. A partnership that can last for ever.

part three

Workout Charts

Here are the Workout Charts I promised you. They can be copied or used as a basis to make your own Workout Charts. It is a good idea to work to some kind of format so that you do not forget any number. I never give any of these charts to a client, but only describe where I get a number from and to what it relates.

Birth Number

Enter the date of birth and work out the number:

Birth Date   ..↓......./......./........
........↓......./......./........
↓......./......./........
Now we add across: →   ......+......+........♥ ____(**Birth Number**)

Whole Name Number

Alphabet Pad

1	2	3	4	5	6	7	8	9
A	B	C	D	E	F	G	H	I
J	K	L	M	N	O	P	Q	R
S	T	U	V	W	X	Y	Z	

Consonant/Vowel Pad

```
     1      5      9         6         3    5    7
     A B C D E F G H I J K L M N O P Q R S T U V W X Y Z
     2 3 4  6 7 8  1 2 3 4 5  7 8 9 1 2  4 5 6 7 8
```

Whole Name Number Workout Chart

Enter names and work out the numbers

```
.................... +............................ +............................ =«...» /...
.................... /............................ / .............................. .↑....
.................... /............................ / .............................. .↑....
Name_____ /_____ /_____ ↑↓
.................... /............................ / .............................. ↓
.................... /............................ / .............................. ↓
.................... /............................ / .............................. ↓
.................... +............................ +............................ .↓=«...» /...↓
```

Consonant Number ⇑..↓

Add **Vowel** & **Consonant Numbers** between«...» together and reduce«...» /◆.....

Whole Name Number ⇑

................./.................. **Given Names Totals**

Add the **Vowel** & **Consonant Numbers** of each name separately and write them in the space above

Birthday Number

The birthday number (actual day on which the subject was born): _____

Maturity Number

Bring down the unreduced Birth Number (marked ♥ in the Birth Number chart above), and the unreduced Whole Name Number (marked ◆ in the Whole Name Number chart above):

.......♥ + ...◆ = ...(now reduce this number) = ...(Maturity Number)

Changed Name Number

Changed Name . . . .

. . . . = .../ . . . .

Bring down the first and second name numbers from the original **Name Number Chart**

First Name No. . . . .+ . . . . .Second Name No. . . . .+ **Changed Name**

Number . . . . . . = ...= . . . . . .

Give a **Changed Name Number** of ⇑

Early Development Number

Add up the letters of the first name:

. . . .= . . . . **Early Development Number**

Early Lesson Number

Day . . . .   Month . . . .   Year . . . .

. . . .

. . . .

Subtracting the lesser from the greater:

Day = ...

Month = ...

= . . . .

Then we take number of the month and the year, and again subtract the lesser from the greater:

Month = ...

Year = ...

= . . . .

Now take the lesser from the greater of these two numbers:

. . . . ⁻ . . . . = ...

Early Lesson Number = ...

Karmic Debt Number

Check which numbers have a Karmic Debt on them, particularly Birth Number, Whole Name Number, Vowel and Consonant Numbers. Remember these Karmic Debt indicators are 13/4, 14/5, 16/7 and 19/1.

- Birth Number:
- Whole Name Number:
- Vowel Number:
- Consonant Number:
- Maturity Number:

Karmic and Second Time Karmic Lesson Numbers

We find the lessons by the expedient of looking at the numbers in the subject's full name. Then we look to see what numbers are missing between 1 – 9.

Then we must look at the subject's other main numbers:

- Birth Number:
- Whole Name Number:
- Vowel Number:
- Consonant Number:

If a number is missing from all the main numbers as well, then it is a Karmic Lesson Number. If we do find the number elsewhere, then a Second Time Karmic Lesson is in play.

Missing Numbers

Place in the numbers below again and work out what numbers are missing.

- Birth Number:
- Whole Name Number:
- Vowel Number:
- Consonant Number:
- Maturity Number:

Missing Numbers: __/ __/ __/ __/ __/ __

Repeated Numbers

Take the Date of Birth and check which numbers are repeated.

Date of Birth: _____
Repeated Numbers:

1   ...
2   ...
3   ...
4   ...
5   ...
6   ...
7   ...
8   ...
9   ...

Grids

Below is a grid with the squares numbered.

3	6	9
2	5	8
1	4	7

Here are some more grids. Add the arrows yourself once you have filled in the relevant numbers of the person's date of birth or first name.

Date of Birth:

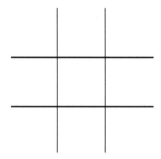

First Name:

Work out the arrow numbers and place them here:
Birth Grids:
First Name Grids:

Personal Year Number

Work out what the Personal Year is. If the Birthday is due soon, it is advisable to give the next year as well.

Day .... /Month .... / Present Year ....
.... /............................/............................
.... /............................/...........................=......=...

Personal Year Number ⇧

Compatibility

You will remember that we do these charts by ratings of how many stars are given: 1* 2** 3*** or 4 ****.

Work out the Birth Numbers of the two people.

First Number is: _____

Second number is: ____

Check Compatibility chart for rating and enter here:

Business: _____

Personal: _____

Sample Workout Charts

★
Marilyn Monroe

Now I am going to show you a chart completely worked out for a very famous person. I have chosen someone who has passed on because any comments can no longer affect her, and also you have some idea of the personality and the complete cycle of her life by which to judge the chart.

I have tried to verify her data as best possible, and trust that to the best of my knowledge it is correct. My apologies if any information is not right.

Here are the Workout Charts for her Numbers, filled in.

Birth Number

Birth Date   ..↓....1.../...6..../...1926
                  ..↓....1../...6..../..18...
                  ↓....1.../...6..../....9..
Now we add across: →   ....1...+....6...+.....9. = 16 ♥ 7 (**Birth Number**)

Whole Name Number

Name Chart   **Vowel Number** ⇓

.....7............. +...........6............. +...........8............. =«..21.» /3
.....7............. /...........6............. / ....17............. ..↑....
6.........1....... /...........5..1........... /....6.......5.........6....↑....
Name N O R M A   /   J E A N   /M O R T E N S O N↑↓
5.....9..4....... /...........1..........5......... / 4.....9..2.....5...1.....5 ↓
...18............. /...........6........... / ....26........ .↓
...9............. /...........6........... / ....8...........↓
....9............. +...........6........... + ...8........... =«23» / 5↓

                                                   Consonant Number ⇈..↓

Add **Vowel** & **Consonant Numbers** between«..» together and reduce«...44...» /..8

                                                   Whole Name Number ⇈

...7 + 9 = 16 = 7..../........6 + 6 = 12 = 3..... **Given Names Totals**

Add the **Vowel** & **Consonant Numbers** of each name separately and write them in the space above

Birthday Number

Marilyn's Birthday Number was **1**

Maturity Number

16♥ + 44♦ = 60 = **6**

Changed Name Number

Changed Name ....B....A....K....E....R
                    ....2....1....2....5....9......= ...19....../.....1....

Bring down the first and second name numbers from the original **Name Number Chart**

First Name No......7....+.....Second Name No. .....3....+ **Changed Name Number** ...1...= ... 11 ...= 11

Give a **Changed Name Number** of ⇈

Changed Name ....D..I..M..A..G..G..I..O

.....4...9...4....1...7...7...9...6.. = ...47....../.....11....

Bring down the first and second name numbers from the original **Name Number Chart**

First Name No......7....+.....Second Name No. .....3....+ **Changed Name**

Number ...11...= ... 21 ...=....3

Giving a **Changed Name Number** of ⇑

Changed Name ....M..I..L..L..E..R

....4..9..3...3...5...9.............. = ..33../6

Bring down the first and second name numbers from the original **Name Number Chart**

First Name No......7....+.....Second Name No. .....3....+ **Changed Name**

Number ...6...= ... 16 ...=....7

Giving a **Changed Name Number** of ⇑

Changed Name ....M..A..R..I..L..Y..N....M..O..N..R...O...E

....4...1...9..9..3...7..5......4...6...5...9...6...5. = ..73../10/1

Giving a **Changed Name Number** of ⇑

Note

There was another marriage but data for it could not be found.

Early Development Number

Add up the letters of the first name:

N O R M A
5 6 9 4 1 = 25 = **7**

Early Lesson Number

Day...1....	Month...6....	Year..1926.....
.......1...	...........6....	..........18.....
.......1...	...........6....	.........9......

Subtracting the lesser from the greater:

Day = ...1...
Month = ...6....
　　　　= 5

Then we take number of the month and the year, and again subtract the lesser from the greater:

Month = ...6....
Year = ...9...
　　　　= 3

Now take the lesser from the greater of these two numbers:

...5...−...3...=...2...

Early Lesson Number = ...2...

Karmic Debt Numbers

Check which numbers have a Karmic Debt on them, particularly Birth Number, Whole Name Number, and Vowel and Consonant Numbers. Remember these numbers are 13/4, 14/5, 16/7 and 19/1.

● Birth Number: 16/7

● Whole Name Number: 44/8

● Vowel Number: 21/3

● Consonant Number: 23/5

● Maturity Number: 60/6

Karmic and Second Time Karmic Lesson Numbers

We find the lessons by the expedient of looking at the number in our full name. Set the name out like this:

NORMA JEAN MORTENSON
5 6 9 4 1　1 5 1 5　4 6 9 2 5 5 1 6 5
Numbers present: 1, 2, 4, 5, 6, 9
Numbers missing: 3, 7, 8

Now we must look at Marilyn's other main numbers:

- Birth Number: 7
- Whole Name Number: 8
- Vowel Number: 3
- Consonant Number: 5

Karmic Lessons: None
    Second Time Karmic Lessons: 3, 7, 8

Missing Numbers

Place in the numbers below again and work out what numbers are missing:

- Birth Number: 7
- Whole Name Number: 8
- Vowel Number: 3
- Consonant Number: 5
- Maturity Number: 6

Missing Numbers: 1, 2, 4, 9

Repeated Numbers

Date of Birth: 1/6/1926
Frequency of the Numbers:

1	2
2	1
3	0
4	0
5	0
6	2
7	0
8	0
9	1

Grids

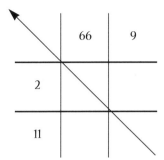

Date of Birth Grid

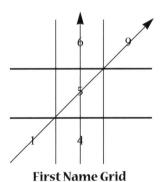

First Name Grid

Birth Grid: Grid 2A Negative
First Name Grid: Grid 1 Positive, Grid 7 Positive

Personal Year

I've worked out the Personal Year for Marilyn's last year of life.

Day ....1........... /Month......6........... / Present Year...1962...
...........1........... /..............6........... / ....18......
...........1........... /..............6........... / ....9........= .16 ./ .7

Personal Year Number ⇑

Compatibility

You will remember that we do these charts by ratings of how many stars are given: 1* 2** 3*** or 4****.

Birth Number: 16/7
Birth number for Arthur Miller: 16/7
First Number is: 7
Second number is: 7
Check Compatibility chart for rating and enter here:
Business: *
Personal: ****

Marilyn's Read-outs

That's the Workout Charts filled in! Below, to save you time, I have pulled out the relevant paragraphs from this book describing what it all means.

Birth Number 7
Contemplative – Mystical – Philosophical – Intellectual

'Different' is the word for 7s. You think and act differently, making it very hard for others to understand you – in fact, do you understand yourself? Even with all your introspective thinking, analysing and contemplation, it's odds on you don't. Lovely fey people, 7s, with a touch of the mysterious about them, as if viewing a world others cannot see – and that's just what they may be doing! You are likely to live in a world of your own making, but beware you don't completely lose touch with the everyday world.

In negativity, you can be distant, sarcastic and at times moody. At worst, a 7 can become completely dissociated from reality and rambling in speech.

In positivity, your deep search for wisdom can benefit all of humanity. Your relationships are very deep and meaningful. You are very intuitive, with perceptive qualities.

'How deep is the ocean?' Probably not deeper than a 7. Much time is taken up thinking, studying and making sense of the world about you. You are a grand dreamer of spectacular dreams, but usually not someone who will actually do something about them. You are not very adaptable, especially to the modern world, although you may make use of technology that is useful to your purposes. You like to spend a lot of time alone. 7s are the philosophers, poets and scholars of this life, not too worried about material gain. They can survive on very little.

Don't fear loneliness or failure or you will find life very difficult. Solitary as you are, you do need some recognition to function well, but learn to operate even if it does not come. You are on track if you are finding the deep truths of life, then offering them, with great humility, to others.

Spiritual Read-out on (the Governing Factor of) Birth Number 7

The governing factor of your spiritual life is that of inspiration. 7s are very sensitive and are often aware of higher consciousness without any suggestion from anybody else. They should seek that still small voice within, for from there will come all answers to their problems and, more importantly, inspiration of a higher nature. This can manifest as mediumistic qualities and, used in the right way, can lead to explanations of the universe which all humanity can share in.

This inner gift can also manifest by way of artistic creativeness such as painting, creating music or writing poetry. Any of these can lead others towards their inner self.

Great care must be taken within all this introspection not to be fooled by illusion. This may take the form of possessions, which come to mean too much to you. This is the lower end of this vibration and can lead to despondency, moodiness and criticism of others. There can also be a chance of thinking oneself better than the rest because of the revelations one might have received. Spiritual snobbery is just as bad as the material kind.

This wonderful vibration, used positively, can demonstrate higher awareness more than any other, for 7s are a link between heaven and earth.

7s nearly always have a purpose in coming to earth, but they can get lost in meditative grandeur and forget it. They may also be asked to make a great sacrifice somewhere in order to fulfil this purpose.

Whole Name Number 8

Self-discipline and mastery of self are what your potential is all about. You have to learn to work really hard, never give up when things look bleak, and achieve success by dint of your own efforts. Your potential is to be business-orientated, capable of running your own show, be it large or small. If you learn judgement of money situations, you could handle large sums of money with flair and ease. Character assessment could come just as easily to you.

Don't become materialistic to the exclusion of all else, or you will cut yourself off from everyone. Being intolerant or over-exacting may bring strain to relationships.

Be the efficient, organized, ambitious, energetic, self-confident and dependable person you are and you will fulfil your mission and destiny and have material success.

The Outer Expression of the Spiritual Self for 8

You will manifest your expression mainly through coming to terms with power, money and restrictions. This may seem highly unspiritual, but you have to learn that the first two of these things are worldly illusions. You also have to learn how to retain thoughts of higher things while seemingly lost in materiality. Try to use your gains to benefit others.

Any restrictions are put in place to teach you personally to seek beyond them – otherwise there would be no pin-pricks in your seemingly easy life. Some people think this expression just means being very lucky, but they don't understand the lesson behind the acquisition of wealth and power. Use this expression to grow and learn many lessons vital for your future lives.

Vowel Number 3

You delight in making others happy and probably like to make them laugh. You will do this with the aid of your witty and friendly self-expression, usually vocal. But you can express it in other artistic ways such as writing or acting. You will never forget your duty, for this is the lesson you have learned in your previous lives and you will know that you are helping yourself by helping others.

In negativity your talking can be rather compulsive and critical of others. In turn you may be very thin-skinned when criticized yourself. Don't be too easy-going or you will never accomplish anything in this life.

In all this helping of others do not forget about yourself and your needs. You want a nice home with beautiful objects around you and that takes time and energy to get and make. You probably lead a very active social life.

The Spiritual Purpose for 3

The key to higher awareness is through the expression of the joy of living. 3 is the number through which you can learn to communicate happiness and joy in the wonderful things of the spirit. You may use any form of communication to do this, from words to pictures. Do not jump hither and thither too much or you may lose the chance of making definite spiritual progress in this life.

Focus your attention on things of a higher nature and absorb what you learn. It is your job in life to give it out to others in a form which they can understand. Yours is the ability to communicate, so use it to help other people in their search for spirituality.

Consonant Number 5

This represents a secret wish to be sexy, witty and exciting. You would like to be thought of as a great dresser and well-travelled person. Nothing is stopping you, just go out and choose the clothes and stop off at the travel agents to pick up a few leaflets. Freedom can be yours, with a little effort.

Inner Spiritual Personality for 5

This number shows that you have an ability to demonstrate constructive freedom. Many think freedom means not having anything to do. You can show that it is much more than that. It is the freedom to choose to do what is necessary to help your fellow man and raise your own consciousness.

Birthday Number

1	Positive	Having new ideas, resolute, inventive and creative, self-dependent
	Negative	Jealous, dominating

Maturity Number 6

You are likely to have to learn to cope with responsibilities, probably of a family nature. This will bring love and affection to the fore, and making use of caring as a means of expressing this love. This lesson will round out your abilities to show love in maturity.

Changed Name Numbers

Changed Name Number 11

Your new name modifies your vibrations by developing illumination, a gift from a higher plane than most. If this is also your Birth Number then you are trying to strengthen this characteristic. But beware it does not drive you into the negative, namely being too dreamy.

    Keyword: *Illumination* – and nervous tension may be introduced on this vibration. Intuition should be developed and there must be a readiness to mediate between heaven and earth. Inspire others by your own illumination.

Changed Name Number 3

Your new name modifies your vibrations by developing communication, the ability to express yourself in creative ways. If this is also your Birth Number then you are trying to strengthen this characteristic. But beware it does not drive you into the negative, namely being introverted.

    Keyword: *Joy of living* – which you have to make others see through your art, writing, speech or acting, some way that will express the wonder and joy of being alive. In a simple form it may just be talking to a friend or neighbour.

Changed Name Number 7

Your new name modifies your vibrations by developing understanding, giving yourself time for introspective thought. If this is also your Birth Number then you are trying to strengthen this characteristic. But beware it does not drive you into the negative, namely being difficult.

    Keyword: *Analysis* – thought must be given to those things which do not pertain to this world. In this way you can become a more rounded person with some kind of philosophy which will sustain you through life's tribulations.

Changed Name Number 1

Your new name modifies your vibrations by developing individuality and an ability to cope on your own, alone. If this is also your Birth Number then you are trying to strengthen this characteristic. But beware it does not drive you into the negative, namely selfishness.

Keyword: *Individualization* – this does not mean selfishness but learning to be yourself and not relying on others. Inner strength to survive can be found within this vibration. But, as mentioned, beware it does not drive you into the negative.

Early Development Number 7

With this Early Development Number you will learn to live the life within the self. You must trust the direction that intuition leads you; it is for your own growth. You must find that time spent alone is anything but wasted, indeed is the most profitable way of spending it. In these times alone you can find wisdom and truth derived from meditation and study. All this should help bring peace to your soul and a realization that money and material matters are as nothing set against this inner peace.

Early Lesson Number 2

In childhood you could have been lacking in self-confidence, been rather put upon by others and given the run around. You would have been compliant due to not wishing to get hurt by the words or actions of others. You may have shunned the company of others even though you wished you could be with them. In other words, in childhood you could have been ultra-sensitive to what others thought about you or said to you.

This is the negative of being sensitive to others' needs, and should have turned to the positive expression of the 2 vibration by adulthood. It can be a tool to bring out intuitive awareness of what another person and their feelings are all about.

Karmic Debt 16/7

A Karmic Debt has come about because of a tendency in past lives to become involved in love affairs of a doubtful nature – that is, ones that were often unusual, illicit, strange or bizarre. What is sure is that, unfortunately, you did not behave towards your partner in the best way. You could have caused hurt, suffering or shame, and certainly would not have shown responsibility.

This will have left you in this life exhibiting the negative traits of the 7, making you a difficult person to approach – usually because your outward actions disconcert others so they often up and leave you alone. You may also play on your 'differentness' to a point of being awkward. Being a 7, this gets a reaction from you of 'oh well, I want to be alone anyway.' Not true, you like and need loving companionship as much as the next person. Isolation can be taken too far. Yet you will find it difficult to keep relationships of a permanent nature going.

When this debt is found in a Birth Number it can cause much impermanence in life. Things seem to come, but more important they go – with monotonous regularity. Sudden changes happen which can leave you devastated, and which don't seem to happen to other people. Indeed, people will often think there must be something wrong with you, yet you know it was fate at work. Deceptions and losses are common occurrences with this number. Sometimes you are at a loss to know what it is that you have done to deserve this continual reversal of fortune.

What can be done to regain soul balance? Well, quite often you are the cause of your own undoing even if it does seem to be fate. Be honest with yourself and explore this possibility. The greatest way to counteract these trials is to devote your life to loving and serving in selfless ways. Put your own needs last. You must find faith in yourself and accept the changes, using them to grow. If you do not and you exhibit too much pride, things will only get worse. Accept the impermanence and flow with it. Although you may remember nothing of what has led to this debt, it is quite possible that you have, even in this life, continued to act in the same manner, particularly in youth. Now you are seeking to understand yourself and things even greater than yourself. Often the people you hurt in past lives are still around you in your present life, so you never know when you may have the chance to repay your debt by selfless service to others.

Second Time Karmic Lessons

Second Time Karmic Lesson 3

There may be some difficulties with expressing yourself in your social encounters. You may not be too good at putting yourself over to others. You must work hard on expressing your feelings and building confidence in your ability to express yourself. Make the 3s in your other numbers work for you.

Second Time Karmic Lesson 7

This means that in this life you will come to appreciate things unseen as well as seen. There can be a realization that the non-material world is just as real as the material, and lead to you having longer-lasting values. Indeed, spiritual values will mean more to you as life goes on, and can finally bring deep joy and peace.

Second Time Karmic Lesson 8

You may be slightly out of balance in the way you approach money in your life. This may cause problems in other areas of your life. Because you have an 8 in your other numbers you will probably be aware of this already. You must learn how to deal with money and/or dependence on others.

Missing Numbers

Missing Number 1

Be much more assertive. Make people sit down and listen to what you are saying. Take control and lead the way more. Dare to live to the full. Pick one thing to start with and seek excellence. With confidence gained, move on to full control of self and others.

Missing Number 2

You are possibly being too much of an individual and not co-operating too well with others. Team work is important, so try to show more sympathy and tolerance. Sometimes in life one must take a back seat and let others shine.

Missing Number 4

Is discipline a little lacking here? Build yourself some strong foundations and bring a bit of order into your life. It will benefit any task you have to tackle. Learn to handle your money better as well, then everything should go more smoothly.

Missing Number 9

Philanthropy is not just a long word, it means the world does need your help. Your example may make others care as well, so start caring and sharing. Don't live with tunnel vision, you could be much more expansive if you tried.

Repeated Numbers

Two 1s

You are able to put things into words easily, and your way of looking at life is well balanced.

One 2

Not good when in competition with others. Do not like criticism and easily hurt.

Two 6s

Over-love of home. Beware of getting too house-proud – home is a place to relax.

One 9

What you've got is good! Nothing in life is perfect.

Grids

Birth Grid

Grid 2A: Missing 3-5-7 (Negative Characteristics)

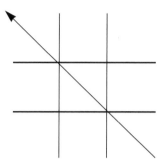

Things metaphysical are not trusted. Understanding of human nature could be better. A large streak of scepticism here, loss of faith, distrust and suspicion.

First Name Grids

Grid 1: Possessing 1-5-9 (Positive Characteristics)

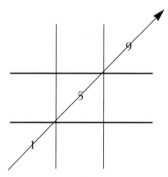

Strong and continued intentions. Great purpose and patience in all you do. Able to concentrate and show persistence and determination. Showing devotion.

Grid 7: Possessing 4-5-6 (Positive Characteristics)

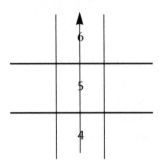

Likely to have hopes and dreams, and the strength to make them come true. A need to possess here and likely to have wants and needs, even cravings for things that give pleasure, sometimes for the self but also for others.

Year Read-out 7

Introspection is the name of the game in a 7 year. Time to attend to the inward person. Take time to contemplate just what this world, and maybe the next, is all about. Others might find you a bit withdrawn this year, but you are just preparing the way for next year, clearing the decks and laying down the ground-work for possible business expansion.

Meanwhile develop your own inner faith in yourself and an awareness of higher things. Put yourself through a health-check.

Compatibility

7 with 7

Business: *
Personal: ****
Blissful – 7 being the only other one who can understand another 7. With both of you somewhat out of this world, business together could be a disaster. Even your own material needs will suffer if you don't come down to earth. Ideas alone will not feed you, but what beautiful music of the spheres you listen to together.

✶
Marilyn's Syntheses

Now you have all the data. If you have read through the paragraphs above you will probably have noted some very remarkable numbers in this chart. You may well be on the way to understanding the lady a bit better. What I usually do now is to pull out the numbers in a certain way to see if there is a pattern. I do it like this:

First I bring all the numbers together:

- Birth Number: 16/7
- Whole Name Number: 44/8
- Vowel Number: 21/3
- Consonant Number: 23/5
- Maturity Number: 60/6
- Early Development Number: 7
- Early Lesson Number: 2
- Changed Name Numbers: first 11, second 1, third 3, fourth 7
- Birthday Number: 1
- Karmic Debts: One on Birth Number (16/7)
- Karmic Lessons: None
- Second Time Karmic Lessons: 3, 7, 8

Now I 'plot' these numbers, as in the list below:

1s: 1   2s: 1
3s: 2   4s: 0
5s: 1   6s: 1
7s: 4 (one karmic debt)   8s: 2
9s: 0
11s: 1   22s: 0

Of Further Interest

Grids	2A Neg, 1 Pos, 7 Pos
Personal Year	7
Compatibility	7 with 7
Missing Numbers	1, 2, 4, 9

With this layout it is easier to spot the Hard and Soft Numbers and the Harmonies and Conflicts.

A pattern emerges, in this case the preponderance of 7s! But by far, the most interesting fact is the Karmic Debt of 16/7 on Marilyn's Birth Number. The first line in our chart for this Karmic Debt reads *A Karmic Debt has come about because of a tendency in past lives to become involved in love affairs of a doubtful nature – that is, ones that were often unusual, illicit, strange or bizarre.* And later – *This will have left you in this life exhibiting the negative traits of the 7.* Further it says – *Although you may remember nothing of what has led to this debt, it is quite possible that you have, even in this life, continued to act in the same manner, particularly in youth.*

It does seem that Marilyn continue to stay in the negative of 16/7 for her life – that is, she continued to act in the same manner as caused her to have a Karmic Debt. Her relationships were quite bizarre and she was unable to settle down with one particular person. I wonder if it would have helped if she had known about the Debt? Perhaps not, for she hid from the 7-ness which, we must note, she took on 4 times in her numbers. One does not see much of the 'mystical' or 'psychic' coming to the fore. But in other ways one can see the 7 having its effect. Differentness, and introspection, and in the negative a great deal of time taken up with the representation of the self to the world. A rather shallow side of a 7 interested in clothes and beauty.

The knocks and changes certainly made themselves felt in her life. A terrible childhood, a difficult mother, many marriages, and bizarre affairs. Yet such great success. How come? I think this is explained by the Whole Name Number, the second most important number in a chart. Marilyn's was 8, which you will recall is material success. There is no doubt that she dedicated herself to success in her chosen profession and attained fame and fortune. But at what price? A hard and soft number plus the exact opposites – 7, the unseen world, and 8, the seen world. Yet I feel she came to earth to try to understand the 7 energy.

Why the choice of acting as the method to gain this success? That is explained by the third most important number, the Vowel Number, which is the number of communication, a 3. This was strengthened by an extra 3 vibration when she married Joe DiMaggio, the famous baseball player.

Her life was further complicated by a Maturity Number of 6, which would have made the desire for a family, love and responsibility come to the fore. I think this is seen in her marriage to Arthur Miller, the playwright, which is numerologically interesting in itself – he also has a Karmic Debt 16/7 on his Birth Number, and it again gave Marilyn a vibration of 16/7 in her changed name. When you see this kind of chart you know something pretty strong is going on karmically.

Indeed, the number of changes to Marilyn's name would have made her very uncomfortable. That many veils being put on and lifted off would have tended to mix up all her energies and make them unclear. But her main change, from Norma Jean Mortenson to Marilyn Monroe, is a 1. This combined with the 8 helped her to the stardom she so assiduously sought.

Marilyn must have done some work on her Karmic Lessons, as all three are Second TIme Karmic Lessons. The interesting point is that they are 3, 7 and 8, which correspond with her first three main - numbers intensifying the energy here.

A most important Grid to notice in this chart is 2A Negative on her date of birth. You will recall that the reading for this says – *Things metaphysical are not trusted. Understanding of human nature could be better. A large streak of scepticism here, loss of faith, distrust and suspicion.* I have often found this grid in people who have come to understand 'things metaphysical' – and I feel that they take on this Grid to put the cat among the pigeons. It often sparks their interest in such things. Now it may have been that Marilyn was into 'things metaphysical' and that I just haven't read or heard anything about this side of her. Hollywood stars are often interested in astrology, or go to consult mediums. Show business has a reputation for its interest in Spiritualism and New Age matters. But I haven't seen much on this interest in her profiles, so for all that she tried so hard to come to understand her 7-ness I don't think it worked. As I say, she may have kept an interest in such things quiet. However, generally the energy of her Karmic Debt 16/7 seems to have overwhelmed her, and it is a disheartening fact numerologically that she died in a Personal Year of 16/7.

As mentioned before, I picked this person because most people know her story. It has fascinated many and will continue to do so in the future, I am quite sure. But this is the chart of an extraordinary woman. Sometimes you will find a chart that has rare and strange qualities. Someone who has all the same numbers, or a majority of one number. Or they take on quantities of Karmic Debts and Lessons. But mostly there is just a quiet interchange of numbers which a soul has chosen to experience – you, as a numerologist, can help them to understand themselves and find the right path for them to tread so that they may succeed in their chosen lessons.

✶
Sai Baba

Here is a chart for a well-known spiritual leader in India called Sai Baba. He changed his name, so we start off with his name at birth: Satyanarayana Raja. He was born on the 23/11/1926. Here I will only give the main chart read-outs. There are no Karmic debts.

Birth Number 7
Contemplative – Mystical – Philosophical – Intellectual

'Different' is the word for 7s. You think and act differently, making it very hard for others to understand you – in fact, do you understand yourself? Even with all your introspective thinking, analysing and contemplation, it's odds on you don't. Lovely fey people, 7s, with a touch of the mysterious about them, as if viewing a world others cannot see – and that's just what they may be doing! You are likely to live in a world of your own making, but beware you don't completely lose touch with the everyday world.

In negativity, you can be distant, sarcastic and at times moody. At worst, a 7 can become completely dissociated from reality and rambling in speech.

In positivity, your deep search for wisdom can benefit all of humanity. Your relationships are very deep and meaningful. You are very intuitive, with perceptive qualities.

'How deep is the ocean?' Probably not deeper than a 7. Much time is taken up thinking, studying and making sense of the world about you. You are a grand dreamer of spectacular dreams, but usually not someone who will actually do something about them. You are not very adaptable, especially to the modern world, although you may make use of technology that is useful to your purposes. You like to spend a lot of time alone. 7s are the philosophers, poets and scholars of this life, not too worried about material gain. They can survive on very little.

Don't fear loneliness or failure or you will find life very difficult. Solitary as you are, you do need some recognition to function well, but learn to operate even if it does not come. You are on track if you are finding the deep truths of life, then offering them, with great humility, to others.

Spiritual Read-out on (the Governing Factor of) Birth Number 7

The governing factor of your spiritual life is that of inspiration. 7s are very sensitive and are often aware of higher consciousness without any suggestion from anybody else. They should seek that still small voice within, for from there will come all answers to their problems and, more importantly, inspiration of a higher nature. This can manifest as mediumistic qualities and, used in the right way, can lead to explanations of the universe which all humanity can share in.

This inner gift can also manifest by way of artistic creativeness such as painting, creating music or writing poetry. Any of these can lead others towards their inner self.

Great care must be taken within all this introspection not to be fooled by illusion. This may take the form of possessions, which come to mean too much to you. This is the lower end of this vibration and can lead to despondency, moodiness and criticism of others. There can also be a chance of thinking oneself better than the rest because of the revelations one might have received. Spiritual snobbery is just as bad as the material kind.

This wonderful vibration, used positively, can demonstrate higher awareness more than any other, for 7s are a link between heaven and earth.

7s nearly always have a purpose in coming to earth, but they can get lost in meditative grandeur and forget it. They may also be asked to make a great sacrifice somewhere in order to fulfil this purpose.

Whole Name Number 9

Selflessness and humanitarianism are what your potential is all about. You must learn temperance, forgiveness and sacrifice, and be ready to take anything the world can throw at you. You also have to develop the philanthropic touch and the potential to inspire others by your own works and deeds.

If you turn your back on this difficult potential, by lack of involvement, you can be self-centred, selfish, insensitive and unaware of others' needs and feelings. You can acquire an aloof attitude which makes it difficult for other people to love you, when that is what you really want. Be the idealistic, compassionate, tolerant, broad-minded, loving and generous person you are and you will fulfil your mission and destiny: *to inspire others by the ideal life you lead.*

The Outer Expression of the Spiritual Self for 9

You will manifest your expression mainly through humanitarianism. Some people call this 'do-gooding', but they have not realized the opportunities for spiritual advancement that comes through this lovely vibration of selfless giving.

So go ahead and love the world; it needs all your help and attention. Let love flow out from you so that others may see the joy of giving and follow your example.

A word of warning, though. 9s can have a highly volatile temperament; you must learn to control it at all times. You must also learn not to give and give until you are drained. This does no good at all. Conserve your energies for the most important work – there certainly is plenty out there for you to do.

Vowel Number 8

You can be called on in this life to handle very large events and run great organizations. You can do this, for in your previous lives you have drummed up enough ambition. Now you must use it to drive you on to sustained effort. You are likely to want power, status, riches and success, and they could very well be yours for the taking, and keeping.

In negativity you could be too domineering and expect too much of other people. Your constant striving for material success can exclude thoughts of anything, or anyone, else. Sad, for you are the loser, you are here to learn that other people have needs and emotions.

If you learn this lesson well it will benefit you, for then you can bring out what is best in them. Be wholehearted to gain the rewards of life.

The Spiritual Purpose for 8

The key to higher awareness is through self-discipline and control. The 8 is the number through which you learn this control. Although it is the number of monetary gain and material success, you have to learn iron control of your circumstances, and this in turn can be applied to your inner life. When defeated, you can learn to accept losing gracefully. In success you can learn to use your success to benefit others and lead them.

Be ready, 8s, for anything life can throw at you – it probably will! You are here to learn to cope and pass through testing situations which are your initiation into the life spiritual.

Consonant Number 1

This represents the secret wish that what you would like to be a cool, calm and collected individual, able to handle everything and everyone with ease and poise. You would like to be seen to be an impeccable dresser and be thought of as somebody who really knows what's what and who's who. It takes some very hard work, but this wish could come true.

Inner Spiritual Personality for 1

This number shows that you have an ability to be individual and stand on your own. You do not always need to have a leader and could even become the leader yourself in certain circumstances. Have confidence in your own enlightenment.

Maturity Number 9

You are likely to have to learn the lesson that selfless giving gives great satisfaction in itself. Humanitarian pursuits will attract you, and if you give willingly of yourself you may find a wonderful joy in your mature life. This is a lesson for the higher nature and can be very difficult.

Changed Name Number 11

New name, Sai Baba.

    Keyword: *Illumination* – and nervous tension may be introduced on this vibration. Intuition should be developed and there must be a readiness to mediate between heaven and earth. Inspire others by your own illumination.

I know that these numbers come from a translation of Sai Baba's name, but it is interesting to note their spirituality. Only the 8 is material, but this man has drawn to his charitable work millions of Rupees. He is said to live a very simple life himself, so he seems to know the lesson of 8.

- Birth Number: 7
- Whole Name Number: 9
- Vowel Number: 8
- Consonant Number: 1

- Maturity Number: 9
- Changed Name Number: 11

He starts out a 7 – different and psychic. He is probably one of the best psychics in the world. He expresses it by giving it away through teaching and in actual physical help such as schools, universities and hospitals. As mentioned, the 8 brings the wherewithal. 1 is leadership, and again another 9 to bring a further humanitarian objective. Then, to crown it all, his changed name brings him the mystic Master Number 11.

Gandhi

Here is another man, who is perhaps better known to most than Sai Baba but also Indian: Mohandas Karamchandi Gandhi. This time I will give you the numbers and you can work out a syntheses.

- Date of birth: 2/10/1869
- Name: Mohandas Karamchandi Gandhi
- Birth Number: 9/9
- Whole Name Number: 12/3
- Vowel Number: 12/3
- Consonant Number: 36/9
- Maturity Number: 50/5
- Birthday Number: 2
- Early Development Number: 3
- Early Lesson Number: 6

No Karmic debts or lessons of any kind! Humanitarian, communicative and free at maturity – very interesting.

Birth Numbers of Significant Figures Past and Present

Do you remember those dates of births I gave you to work out in the chapter on Birth Numbers (*page 5*)? Well, here they are with the Birth Number and who they are:

5/5/1818	Karl Marx: 1
15/8/1950	Princess Anne: 2
3/12/1923	Maria Callas: 3
15/4/1452	Leonardo Da Vinci: 4
6/8/1881	Sir Alexander Fleming: 5
14/3/1879	Albert Einstein: 6
30/11/1874	Sir Winston Churchill: 7
25/10/1881	Pablo Picasso: 8
22/2/1857	Lord Baden Powell: 9
27/1/1756	Wolfgang Amadeus Mozart: 11
18/6/1942	Paul McCartney: 22

I have tried to make them internationally known people so you may judge their characters. Karl Marx – a leader and pioneer in a new philosophy. Princess Anne – a diplomat. Maria Callas – communication (you will find that many singers are 3s). Leonardo Da Vinci, a prolific worker, actually had a Karmic Debt on work. And so on. Here are a few more:

1s

Elizabeth I
Jacques Cousteau

Charlie Chaplin
George Bernard Shaw

All very individual people, leaders in their own field and pioneers of the new.
Prince Henry (or Harry, as he is known) is also a 1.

2s

2s are quite rare. Princess Anne is one of the few public figures who is a 2, and
she does show diplomacy very well. Tony Blair is another – and I feel history
will remember him more for his diplomatic skills than his political ideas.
Mussolini was another – and he must have been very diplomatic to get on
with Hitler!

3s

Enrico Caruso
Salvador Dali
Spike Milligan
Doris Day

Communicators come to the fore here.

4s

Percy Bysshe Shelley
Liam Gallagher
Annie Besant
Queen Elizabeth the Queen Mother

5s

Franklin Delano Roosevelt
Robespierre
Vincent Van Gogh
Russel Grant
Arthur Conan Doyle

Abraham Lincoln
The Kray twins

Interesting that the infamous London gangsters the Krays lost their freedom with their prison sentence. Abe Lincoln personifies the constructive freedom of the 5.

6s

Agatha Christie
Teilherd du Chardin
Charles De Gaulle
Esther Ranson
Richard Nixon
Adolf Hitler

I once heard Esther Ranson say on the radio 'I ask myself have I got the balance right?' and 'I hate being alone.' Typical 6 things. On the negative side of 6 we have Richard Nixon and Hitler!

7s

Lewis Carroll
Louis Pasteur
Gregory Peck
Queen Elizabeth II
Princess Diana
Jimi Hendrix
J. F. Kennedy
Andy Warhol
Robin Knox Johnston

And many more. Knox Johnston is the lone sailor who wrote a book entitled *A World of My Own* – very 7! And, in case you hadn't worked it out yet, yours truly, the author.

8s

Lyndon B. Johnson
Mohammed Ali
Paul Newman
Peter Sellers
Ammani
Saddam Hussein

9s

Gandhi
Elvis Presley
Brigitte Bardot
William Roach (of *Coronation Street* fame)

11s

Gurdjieff the mystic
Lord Byron
Coco Channel
Bill Clinton
Prince Philip
Prince Charles
Prince William

22s

People with this Master Number for their Birth Number are not easy to find. I have given you Paul McCartney. There is also one that is interesting – former Prime Minister, John Major. He should have been the leader of leaders – but does he back off into the 4 to become the grey man, I ask myself?

Other Ways of Looking at Numerological Numbers

Although I do not tend to use numerology as a predictive science, it can be quite interesting to look at numbers other than those on a person's chart. Such things as house numbers, telephone numbers and so on. I personally don't find they have much relevance, and I certainly don't worry if they're 'lucky' or not.

There can be fascinating revelations in the dates of important world events. For instance, the Birth of the British Empire (that is, the date that the title 'Empress' was given to Queen Victoria) was an 8. Material wealth certainly arose from that. The end of the Second World War in Europe was a 5, as was Nelson Mandela's release from long years in prison. Kennedy's assassination was a 7, and it happened on the 22nd day of the 11th month. Chernobyl was a 9 – the end of an era of thinking that atomic fallout could be limited.

Dates can be viewed in this way, as can any particular year. We covered Personal Years, earlier but each year can have an overall flavour given it by its numerological number. As mentioned before, this has little relevance to an individual but it does lend a tone to life at large. One can expect diplomacy in a 2 year, mysticism in a 7 year, and so on. The number of a year can be found by the simple expedient of adding it together and reducing. The meanings are basically the same as when interpreting any other number. In thinking of numbers in this way, do not forget the 1-9 cycle.

It can be quite rewarding to seek out a famous personage's real name when born and do their complete chart. It is an exercise that will help you gain experience of synthesizing. Also try to do as many charts as possible for people you know personally, so that you may examine the resulting read-outs with them and discover new secrets in their numbers.

This book has been particularly pointed towards knowing the Soul Self, hence its title, *Soul Numerology*. It has tried to show the path the person has chosen, what debts or lessons they have come to deal with or learn and something of the character they have brought with them. This all then reflects on the present character and emotional make-up of the person. It can also give them a 'why' in understanding their own nature and how best to deal with the situation they find themselves in. It is also a reading of the present character – and those not interested in spiritual matters can read it simply for this. Perhaps they cannot – or don't want to – face responsibility for themselves yet.

Soul Numerology means looking yourself in the eye and accepting yourself as you are.

Always give encouragement to the person for whom you have done a chart. Try to find positive as well as negative aspects. Congratulate them if they have beaten some particular negative energy. Most of all, always point out the main Birth Number life-path they have chosen.

✦

Family Numbers: The British Royal Family

Numbers within a family can be interesting to note. One family which the whole world knows at least something about is the British Royal Family. There are some fascinating numerological numbers here. I cite these only as pointers, not to make any comment upon these people.

First, you may have noticed the line of men with 11s. This is a difficult Master Number to cope with – some back off into the 2. This line of 11s actually started quite far back, with Prince Charles' great-grandfather, George V, though it skipped his grandfather George VI (who was a 13/4). Prince Philip is definitely a 'power behind the throne' 2, yet shows glimpses of seeing the higher spiritual dimension of things. Charles again shows much interest in things of a spiritual nature. This can be taken to extremes, as in his dreamy talking to plants. As for William – well, we will just have to wait and see. All three should or could lead people using the knowledge that is within them from many past incarnations – during which they were probably together, or at least connected in some way.

Secondly, there are a lot of Karmic Debts in this family. The first is with Elizabeth, the Queen Mother, who has a 13/4 debt. This is a debt on work, you will remember, one which usually makes the person go on and on working. No one has done her work more devotedly and continuously than this great lady. In her nineties and still going, she will carry on, I suspect, until it becomes impossible. Interestingly, she married George VI when he was Duke of York, and who was another with a Karmic Debt of 13/4. He was thrust into the work of kingship whether he liked it or not until his death.

Their daughter, Queen Elizabeth II, has a 16/7 Karmic Debt. Now, interest in psychic matters is known to run right through this family from the time of Queen Victoria (12/3). Elizabeth's grandfather, George V, was also a 7, but with no Karmic Debt. Elizabeth cannot possibly show any interest in psychic matters in public, as Head of the Church of England. Putting this aside, though, there is still the debt. It seems to have affected her life through others around her. First her uncle, Edward VIII (later the Duke of Windsor), upset the whole family by abdicating as the result of a relationship dilemma (please note that he was a 6: love, balance, family and responsibility). Her whole life changed overnight. This is a typical 16/7 debt change. Later her sister, Princess Margaret (a 15/6) fell in love with an 'unsuitable' (divorced) gentleman. Then came her later marriage to Snowdon, which failed, and the Queen had to face the first divorce in the close family.

The Queen's daughter, Princess Anne, had a marriage that broke up and then a remarriage. Later came the two somewhat bitter breakdowns in the marriages of Princes Andrew and Charles. Again and again the Queen has had to face up to and deal with relationship problems which must have caused her great pain and distress.

Lastly, the two daughters-in-law in question both had Karmic Debts. Sarah, Duchess of York, has a 13/4 debt and will probably have to work hard all her life. The late Diana, Princess of Wales, had a 16/7 debt. Surprise, surprise!. Also she had changes in her life of a sweeping kind.

I think all these women have been connected many times before. Maybe with or without the gentlemen of the family. There is most obviously a great deal of Karma flying around here which does not make for an easy life despite their riches.

Through numerology we can see patterns within a person's family, relationship and friendships. Anything which offers us an explanation of the trials and tribulations of this world must be worthwhile, for it gives us a clue on how to deal with the situations in which we find ourselves.

For those who have followed me thus far through the book, thank you and I hope you have enjoyed it. Please do not stop here, this is merely a starter book. There is much more to numerology that is equally fascinating. I have listed in Recommended Reading books which I have found helpful and informative, some simple, some more advanced. I trust your new knowledge will help you, and those for whom you do charts, to move forward physically and spiritually to a greater understanding of the energies and vibrations you have come to earth to experience.

Recommended Reading

Unfortunately I cannot guarantee that all these books are still in print or available to buy.

Master Your Vibration – Edmund Harold (Spiritual Venturers' Education Trust, New Zealand)

Numerology: The Complete Guide – Matthew Oliver Goodwin (2 vols; Newcastle Publishing Co. Inc. USA)

Numerology and the Divine Triangle – Faith Javane and Dusty Bunker (Whitford Press [a division of Schiffer Publishing])

The Numerology Handbook – Julia Line (The Aquarian Press)

Numerology and Your Future – Dusty Bunker (Whitford Press)

Principles of Numerology – Sonia Ducie (Thorsons)

Index

Tarot

The complete handbook for the apprentice

Eileen Connolly

This book has established itself as a modern classic on the interpretation of the Tarot. It contains three linked sections to enable students to work with and understand the Tarot cards and their relationship with Astrology, Numerology and the Cabala.

Including:

- basic lessons, exercises, procedures and meditations relating to the Major and Minor Arcana
- guides to the positive and negative interpretations of the symbols on each card
- procedures and spreads for using the cards in divination

Eileen Connolly stresses the importance of becoming directly involved with the symbolism of the Tarot, rather than just learning the meanings by rote. This handbook will be an excellent guide and point of reference as you progress swiftly and safely towards a deep knowledge of the subject.

Seventy-Eight Degrees of Wisdom

A book of Tarot

Rachel Pollack

Together in one volume for the first time, the classic texts that helped launch the modern Tarot renaissance.

Described by many as 'the Bible of Tarot readers', the two volumes of *Seventy-Eight Degrees of Wisdom* brought awareness of myth and modern psychology to the Tarot's ancient esoteric symbolism, and have inspired a whole generation of students of the Tarot.

Here, uniquely, the texts for *The Major Arcana* and *The Minor Arcana* appear in one volume, specially revised and updated by Rachel Pollack in the light of her thirty years' teaching, reading and writing about Tarot cards.

'Rachel Pollack's *Seventy-Eight Degrees of Wisdom* is on my "Top Ten" list of all time Tarot greats! This classic book with never outgrow its usefulness.' Mary K. Greer, author of *Tarot for Yourself: A Workbook for Personal Transformation*.